for Lynn, who somehow keeps me
on the straight and narrow

Phototypeset from the author's disk by Piccadilly Press.
Printed and bound by Creative Print and Design (Wales),
Ebbw Vale, Gwent
for the publishers Piccadilly Press Ltd.,
5 Castle Road, London NW1 8PR

A catalogue record for this book is available
from the British Library

ISBN: 1 85340 515 9

Irene Yates lives in Redditch, Worcs. She was a primary school
teacher, specialising in literacy skills, for sixteen years. She is now
an educational writer and consultant.

PRE-SCHOOL LEARNING FOR PARENTS

Irene Yates

Piccadilly Press • London

CONTENTS

INTRODUCTION

During the first five years of life, your baby will learn more, and at a faster rate, than he/she will ever learn again. These are called the 'formative' years because this is the period when your baby begins to form his or her future role in life. What happens now is the foundation for all that will happen later. How your baby develops, physically, intellectually, socially and emotionally during these years is the stepping stone to all the learning that will follow.

You have an incredibly important part to play in this early development, because *you* are the baby's first teacher. This book sets out to explain the learning process and to show you how you can assist your baby in every area of development. You don't need special equipment or lots of expensive toys to help your child. Mostly what you need is a little knowledge, plenty of enthusiasm and a sensible approach which will help you to observe and understand each pattern of behaviour or stage of learning as your child meets it.

The key to teaching a child is to make every experience as enjoyable and positive as possible. If you are interested and supportive, your home can't fail to be an enriching, stimulating environment. This will give your child confidence and so promote all aspects of his/her development. In their formative years, children are learning something during every moment – you can help to make that learning constructive and beneficial.

Chapter One

PRE-SCHOOL LEARNING

THE UNIQUENESS OF YOUR CHILD

Your child is unique. And if you have more than one, each of your children is unique. You will be able to see this quite clearly for yourself. One child may be placid and even-tempered, another may be tetchy and impatient. One may eat everything that's placed in front of her/him, another may flatly refuse to eat anything but cream-cheese sandwiches. One may be chattering and talking away by two-and-a-half, another may not want to speak a word at three. One may be timid and shy, one may be gregarious and vivacious.

All children are individuals. They have their own genetic endowment and their own traits, patterns of development, and routes to learning. There's a long-running debate about whether nature (what children are born with) or nurture (the way they are treated) is the most important factor in development. The argument will probably never be solved. Even in one family, where nurture might virtually be said to be the same – except for the child's place in the family – children will develop differently.

WHAT ARE STAGES OF DEVELOPMENT?

It stands to reason then, that children within any group will show significant differences in development and learning but will still come within the boundaries of 'normal development'. This is why teachers talk in terms of 'stages of development' rather than in terms of chronological age. What one child can do easily at two-and-a-half another may not do until three – yet another may do at two!

The expression 'stages of development' is a more useful description for teachers than to refer to a child's 'age' because, in most areas of learning, they can break down the stages that children go through to reach the next platform of learning. You can see this clearly if we look at the some of the stages of development a child might pass through in learning to communicate:

Stage 1: The child's first communications are by reflex. It cries to show it is hungry, thirsty, tired, in pain, etc.

Gradually the cries begin to have different tones. You learn to interpret them and understand what each means. The child learns that communication gets results. The child then increases its range of noises, cooing and making little vowel-like sounds of contentment.

Stage 2: The child begins to babble, increasing its range of noises. It begins to make some of the consonant sounds and experiments with them. As the parent babbles back, the baby gets more confident and enjoys the fun even more, thus 'practising' more and more.

Stage 3: The child learns its first one-syllable words – 'Mum', 'Dad', 'drink' – and when the parent says the words back, the child imitates and repeats. With lots of praise and repetition, the child's range of words grows.

Stage 4: The child learns to put two words together. Sometimes there's a gap between the words, so the child says 'Mum . . . drink' and the parent understands that this means, 'You want Mummy to get you a drink?'

Because the parent talks back to the child, filling in the missing words, the child refines its abilities.

Stage 5: The child begins to increase the length of its communications from listening to others until it begins to put three words together – 'Mummy gone work', 'Teddy gone bed', and so on.

Stage 6: The child now uses increasingly complex sentences, and experiments with putting words together rather than just copying or imitating words or phrases.

When Do Stages of Development Happen?

Stages of development don't happen at the same time for all children. They happen because a child has reached a certain level of understanding, or achieved a certain skill or knowledge, and the next stage of development is the natural progression. You can't *push* children into attaining stages of development, but you can *help* them to reach them, by working out exactly what is necessary for the child to get there, and how you can supply that need.

TRY NOT TO PUSH

A word of warning here about *pushing*. Sometimes a child can appear to have made some huge leap-frog when it has been pressured, only to fall back at a later stage. If a stage of development hasn't been completed properly and naturally it's a bit like a house being built without proper foundations. The house may stand up and look OK, but at some point, because a specific part of the foundation isn't there, some of it may crumble.

DO CHILDREN *HAVE* TO GO THROUGH EACH STAGE?

Sometimes children miss out stages of development and that's perfectly OK if they do it for themselves – for instance, a child (who is probably always going to be good at languages) may go from uttering single words to putting sentences together in one fell swoop. This is fine; all you need to do is keep feeding in the vocabulary and enlarging your child's knowledge of language by being a good role model yourself.

A child who is reading may go from recognising shapes straight into learning words – if this is a natural thing for the child to do then she/he has probably absorbed all the knowledge she/he needs to do this in some magical way without you being involved and you just need to carry on from there.

HOW LONG DO THEY STAY AT ONE STAGE?

As with anything else, children learn at different rates. Not only that, but they may have more inclination for one kind of activity than another – for instance, some children may be very physically active and therefore develop good motor control skills more quickly than those who are more cognitive and learn to express themselves more in language.

The important thing is not to hurry children through any stage of development. It's a bit like a piece of string. They need to be there as long as they need to be there. Some children seem to leap from one stage to another without any waiting periods at all; others seem to reach a plateau and stay there for a very long time.

All this is perfectly natural. You can compare it with physical growth. Some children seem to grow in spurts, others in a slow and indefinite way, and the only time you realise they have grown is when something suddenly doesn't fit them any longer.

WHAT DOES THIS MEAN FOR A GROUP?

You can see that if your own children show differences in the ways and the rates that they learn, obviously there will be huge differences within a group of children brought randomly together, for instance at a playschool or nursery.

This is why it is irrational to compare your children with others in any group, to see where they might be lagging behind or where they might be up in front.

Besides, a child who is a shining star in one group may be at the bottom in another, or vice versa. Any group will differ from another because of differences in their circumstances – the social environment for instance, or their resources. This is why the educational establishment is developing a national framework for 'Baseline Assessment'. Baseline Assessment will include what is called 'value-added' information, which will outline differences between the groups which may make a difference to the children's starting point.

The only person you can really safely compare your children with, are themselves. What you are looking for are little steps forward which tell you that they are learning steadily and meeting their potential in all areas.

KNOWING

Before we move on to looking at how children learn, it might be interesting to think about knowledge and the different ways in which we can be said to *know* things.

There are subtle differences between kinds of knowing. For example, there is: knowing that (example – a pencil is a pencil); knowing how (example – to do something); knowing why (example – something happens); knowing what (example – something is for); knowing when (example – it's your turn).

Once you begin to think about what you yourself know, you may be able to add more to this list. Think about whether you learned all these things in the same way. For example, did you learn that the Great Fire of London happened in 1666 in the same way that you learned how to swim? Did you learn that if you tried to walk through a door before you opened it you would hurt yourself, in the same way that you learned when to say 'please' and 'thank you'?

Take this thinking a little bit further and try to work out for yourself exactly how you learned the things described above. Think of something you've learned recently – it may be something like how to use a computer, how to make a spaghetti bolognese, the chronicle of the Hale-Bopp comet – and try to work out how you did it: if possible, aim for three different sorts of knowledge and learning, and try to work out what they were. This will help you to understand how your children learn things.

HOW *DO* CHILDREN LEARN?

Children learn in a variety of ways and, in a way, the way they learn depends upon what they're learning.

COPYING

One of the ways they learn is by *copying* or mimicking. Think back to the description of how children learn language, at the beginning of this chapter. You will remember your children, as babies, cooing at you and trying to repeat the sounds that you made back to them.

By copying or mimicking you, they learn to make the sounds for themselves. They learn how to listen, how to shape their mouths to make specific sounds, and how to use their vocal faculties to make the right sounds back to you.

Babies learn other things by copying – they learn to take turns with you, they learn to wave and do pat-a-cake or other little tasks, they learn to nod and shake their heads for 'no' and 'yes'.

This kind of learning never has a full stop to it. Copying used to be called the 'Sitting next to Nellie' method of learning, because girls working in the cotton mills or other factories often learned to work machines or improve their skills simply by sitting next to some-one and copying them. Learning to knit is a particularly good example of a skill learned by copying.

Copying can also lead to *learned behaviour*. Your children watch as another child throws a tantrum in the supermarket and gets a bar of chocolate as a 'reward' – you and I know it's to shut the child up but . . . The same thing happens again and again. What do your children do? Throw a tantrum – because they've learned that this kind of behaviour wins bars of chocolates.

CONDITIONING

Children learn a great deal through *conditioning*, probably far more than we're ever aware of. It is easiest to explain conditioning in terms of gender. Years ago, children were *conditioned* to their gender roles by their clothing, the toys they were given and the roles that were expected of them.

Thus a little girl was conditioned towards being 'feminine' by wearing pretty, frilly frocks, by being given baby dolls and domestic toys to play with, and by being expected to be 'a good little girl'. Boys were treated very differently. They were expected to be 'big, brave men', they were given toys that people thought were applicable to men, they were dressed in tough clothing that would survive tree-climbing and fights in the mud, they were expected not to cry if they got hurt.

You can condition most animals, or humans, to almost anything. A simple example is that a dog can be conditioned to bark at the door when it wants to come in. It's very easy to teach it – you just give it the reward of opening the door when it barks.

Conditioning happens when your children constantly wake and get out of bed at night. You take them downstairs and give them milk and biscuits to get them back to sleep. What have they learned? That getting out of bed brings rewards. So they do it every night.

Far better to take them by the hand, lead them back to bed, tell them, calmly but firmly, that night-time is for sleeping, and let them know what's expected. So they learn that it's not worth waking up at night.

Conditioning and 'reward' or 'punishment' go hand in hand. If you learn, you are rewarded; if you do not learn, you are punished. 'Reward' can mean anything nice – a smile bestowed, a word of praise. 'Punishment' can, likewise, mean a frown in your direction, a 'tut-tut', a shake of the head. In the early days of state education, children who learned their numbers and letters were told they were 'good', and those who did not, found themselves in trouble. You can see the problem with this kind of teaching and learning. Perhaps a child doesn't have the capacity to learn numbers and letters – should that child be 'punished'? Or helped?

ROTE

Children, in the past, were expected to learn everything by *rote*. This means that you took whatever it was that had to be learned or taught, and repeated it over and over and over again until it became automatic to know it. Many parents and grandparents will remember learning poetry, spelling and times tables in this way. Many will say 'I can still remember that poem today!' or 'I still know all my times tables!'

This may be true, but rote learners also need the right cues to enable them to dredge the automatic response from their memory. They don't necessarily *understand* what's meant by the facts they have learned.

For example, they may know that 8 x 7 = 56 and that it follows 7 x 7 = 49, but they may have no idea that if they had 8 packets of biscuits, each with 7 biscuits, they'd have 56 biscuits. The *facts* they know may have no bearing on their real life at all.

Rote learning was embarked upon in much the same way as conditioning. The children who succeeded were rewarded, and those who failed were punished. But what about the children who don't have a good capacity for remembering – wouldn't they be better helped to try to improve their memory skills, rather than pumped with facts that have no meaning to them?

PRACTICE

Most of our skills are learned by practice. You may come across the occasional person who is so gifted or talented that they only have to do something once and they've 'cracked' it, but most of us have to carry out the same actions repeatedly, in order to perfect them.

Think of learning to drive, or learning to swim. We keep doing it and doing it, going over exactly the same bits, breaking the learning down into stages and continually reinforcing what we are doing right. Within our practice we learn not only what we do right, but what we do wrong, and we eventually manage to eliminate the 'wrong' things. Getting things 'wrong' is a really important part of the learning process. If you don't get things wrong, you can't ever be sure when you are getting them right!

Every time you practise, you are reinforcing good habits, good procedure, and getting better and better at whatever it is you are doing.

Children learn all their skills by practice, from talking or learning to walk, all the way through to reading and writing.

LEARNING THROUGH PLAY

The ideal way for anyone to learn is through play. Play is a natural activity to all animals, not just humans, and you can see animals in the wild practising their social and communication skills by playing with each other.

Play is an excellent way to practise and keep reinforcing all types of learning. For example, children who are absorbed in playing with jugs, bottles and water will be learning all kinds of science and maths. You may think they're just tipping one bottle of water into another over and over again, but what they're learning, amongst other things, is: that water is fluid, that it is wet, that it changes its shape, that different sized and shaped containers can hold different amounts, that if you don't hold the bottle steady you spill the water, that you have to keep your eye on the water going into the bottle as well as on your hand, that you have to hold your wrist in a certain way to pour the water steadily . . . and so on. Of course, if they are indulging in this play activity with another person, they are also learning language and social skills because they're communicating and sharing.

Many educational psychologists believe that play really is the key to learning. You can probably put their theory to the test yourself by setting up an experiment where you try to teach your child something specific (say, the shape of a letter) and do it in a serious way, and then do it again in a 'play' way. Watch for the delight on your child's face when you become actively involved. Which way does your child learn most?

THE IMPORTANCE OF THE SELF-CONCEPT

Possibly the most important factor in any learning that your children do is their concept of themselves: how they actually see themselves, what they believe about themselves. This is because they have to perceive themselves capable of learning before they can learn.

You may have heard the phrase 'self-fulfilling prophecy'. In many cases with children this is exactly what happens – right from the beginning. If children feel valued, loved, worthy and capable of learning, then – assuming no specific problems – they will learn. If they feel unvalued, unloved, unworthy and incapable of learning, they will fail to develop.

Children who have a good self-image, who believe in themselves, will look at the world in a positive light. They will expect to be able to fulfil their own, and your, ambitions. Their hopes for themselves will be in keeping with their abilities, and vice versa – they will expect that they can do all the things they hope to do – therefore, ninety-nine per cent of the time, they will achieve.

Children with poor self-image, who believe themselves to be less smart, less attractive or less able than their siblings or their peers, will see the world in a negative light. They will expect to be disappointed. Almost everything they attempt will go wrong, because they expect it to. And this constant failure will, of course, reinforce their negative self-image.

It's crucial, therefore, that you help your children to

acquire a good self-image right from the beginning. How do you do this?

WHY PRAISE IS IMPORTANT

Teachers know that praise and encouragement are the greatest motivators there can be for children. Actually, praise and encouragement work with adults as well.

Picture yourself learning to drive, or swim or cook. When your efforts went well and you were told that you'd 'behaved' well, you felt a glow of pride and satisfaction inside, which inspired you to greater effort.

This is exactly what happens with children. When you praise them for their efforts (rather than the results) you make them feel valued and appreciated. They feel as if they're 'going in the right direction' and are encouraged to have another go, or try even harder, to make their efforts achieve their goals: they're highly motivated, feel positive, and continue practising. All these are strategies which will lead them to success.

WHY CRITICISM IS UNHELPFUL

Go back to your picture of yourself learning to do something. You make a mistake or do something which, in hindsight, you realise is pretty silly. You're vexed with yourself for being slow. Whoever is leading you shouts at you for getting it wrong. Your motivation is immediately lost. Not only that, but you feel as if it's all too much, it's beyond your capabilities, you're never going to 'get' it. Unless you're very, very lucky, the will to win through disappears. In the worst-case scenario, you give up completely.

Again, this is what happens with children. And once

they get into this negative cycle it is very, very hard to shift them out of it.

They will say to you again and again, 'I can't'. But the worst thing is that this is what they will feel innately, particularly if they are constantly criticised. And once they believe that they cannot, they will not.

What children believe they are, they will become.

KEEPING A BALANCE

Somehow you have to find the balance which is right. It is unhelpful to tell children they are 'brilliant', they are 'wonderful', they are a 'genius', when patently they are not. Far better to keep your praise and encouragement for their actions rather than their personality – for example, instead of saying, 'You're brilliant at drawing,' say, 'You really do work well at your drawing. I can see it getting better and better every day.'

You must have heard people shouting at their badly behaved children: 'You're so naughty! You're a waste of time! You drive me round the bend!' What do you think those children are learning when they are being addressed in this manner repeatedly? And what kind of learning is going on? It doesn't take long to realise that they're being *conditioned* into believing that they are naughty, a waste of time and apt to drive their parents round the bend. What they believe they are, they will be.

Conversely, if you tell your children often enough that they are always a pleasure to take out, that they are polite and well-behaved in company, that everybody enjoys being with them – they will go out of their way to prove you right! Conditioning again!

Remember, it is your *attitude* that will make all the

difference to their self-concept – and, actually, to all their learning.

SKILLS, CONCEPTS AND ATTITUDES

Teachers always talk in terms of skills, concepts and attitudes. Many teachers believe that children are always learning all three all of the time, that none can be learned without the others.

Skills might be explained as *knowing how*. They are the things which we learn to *do*. They include all our motor activities, such as walking, riding a bike, reading, writing etc, and many of our creative activities such as painting, composing poetry or playing an instrument. Skills are *always* learned by practice.

Concepts can be identified as *knowing what* and *knowing that*. They include such things as knowing, for example, that a pencil is a pencil and everything that you could possibly understand about a pencil; understanding numbers; knowing about the world around us; knowing about cause and effect. Concepts can be learned in different ways. They used to be learned by rote but today we try to ensure understanding. Only then can a concept really be said to have been learned.

Attitudes are how you feel about what you are learning. Good attitudes are essential for solid learning and they're affected by lots of things – how the learning is presented, how you feel while you're learning it, whether you have a real inclination to learn it etc. Attitudes affect learning and affect how you will use what you have learned – whether you will remember it or forget it, whether you will make it a part of you.

HOW SKILLS, CONCEPTS AND ATTITUDES WORK TOGETHER

To sum these up, think about yourself in a situation such as learning to swim. The ability to swim is a skill which requires great motor control, so you learn to do it by constant practice. But while you're practising the skill, you're also learning, even if you don't think you are, about the concept of water and body mass – you are becoming aware of how the water moves when you kick, when you float etc. Also, you're learning attitudes, because if your instructor is fierce and over-bearing, if the swimming-pool is crowded and there's no room for you to feel safe, you are probably learning that swimming is something you have to grit your teeth for and conquer. If, conversely, your swimming instructor makes the whole episode great fun, if you have fun and laughter, if you have lots of room and feel safe all the time, swimming will forever be associated in your mind with pleasure and enjoyment and you'll learn it much more easily.

ASSIMILATION

You may remember when you were younger, at school, sometimes coming across something that you found very difficult to understand. Suddenly, the penny seemed to drop and you could say 'Oh, I *get* it now!' (This happens when we're adults too, of course!) This process of 'getting it' is called 'assimilation' and it is only when children have assimilated something that we can actually be sure that they have learned it.

It is almost as though, in assimilating something – a

17

skill, a concept, an attitude, an idea – the children make that something part of their own life, their make-up. The assimilated something becomes part of *them* and, for as long as they need it, it remains theirs.

MOTIVATION

There's another factor involved in the learning process, and that is motivation. Everybody needs motivation to learn. That motivation can come from inside (intrinsic motivation) or outside of you (extrinsic motivation).

Perhaps you want to learn to drive because it's something you want to do for yourself – to conquer it – you want to feel the satisfaction of achievement, you just want to be able to do it. This is intrinsic motivation.

Or perhaps you want to learn to drive because your boss has promised you a top-of-the-range company car when you pass your test. This is extrinsic motivation.

Maybe you want to learn to drive for both reasons. That's fine – the more incentive you have, the more determination you'll find to succeed; the *easier* you will find it to *learn*. Everybody needs some incentive to give them motivation, and you have to find subtle ways of making your child motivated to do things and learn.

THE ONE THING YOU MUST *ALWAYS* DO

Once you are about to embark upon trying to teach your child something, the one thing you must always, always do, is start at the point where your child *is* and not from where you think your child *ought* to be.

This means that you have to find out exactly what

they know, what they can do, what stage of development they are at, and work onwards from there. It's no good expecting, for example, children to climb the ladder of an two metre slide and slide down it, if they are too frightened to stand on the first rung. You have to begin with getting them to step on and step off that first rung until they feel secure and safe. Then move on to the next rung, and so on. You should not worry about the time it takes to achieve small measures of progress, and you should see each step as an achievement in itself and praise it accordingly.

Similarly, it's no good expecting them to do addition and subtraction if they have no concept of numbers or digits. It would be like expecting someone who's only just learned how to switch on the car engine to drive along all the motorways in Britain: all you will do if you get it wrong is *put them off*, probably for ever, so don't ever be afraid to backtrack a little before you begin – in the long run it will save you time, stress and even, possibly, heartache. Keep in mind the maxim 'little steps achieve big journeys'.

PRACTICAL ACTIVITIES

To make sure your teaching and learning sessions aren't stressful, follow these points:
• Think carefully about how you promote your children's self-image – what do they think of themselves, what do they expect of themselves, what do they think you expect of them? Are the levels of expectation realistic for: their stages of development; their abilities; their level of maturity and their grasp

and understanding of the world?

• Think carefully about how you motivate your children. Do you promise them tangible rewards (sweets, toys etc) if they achieve? Could you promise them more subtle rewards (hugs, delight, self-fulfilment) and help them to appreciate them?

• Think about how you feel if your children fail at something you have set as a goal. Are you cross and angry? Can you find a better way into the teaching? Have you thought about the skills, concepts and attitudes involved? Can you break the task down into these and make sure they are all appropriate? Did you begin at a realistic level – where the children *were*? Have you made the task fun? Can you do it in a play way?

• Think about how *you* learn best. Everybody has a preferred learning style. Maybe if you could find out what your own is, it would help you to know how to motivate your child.

• Think of something you really want to help your children to learn. Is it a skill? How can you help them to learn it? Work out a programme before you begin. Decide that you will be encouraging and positive for as long as it takes for them to assimilate. Work out, from their normal behaviour, where they are at to begin with. Begin your programme. Give it lots of time.

• Think about whether you ever allow your children to take the lead. Don't be a *teacher* all the time – let your children tell you what they're really interested in, let them make the choices, don't be over-dominant. Wait and listen, and make your watchword *observation*.

• Observe what they do, what they say, what they like. Observe and adapt to the moment, to your children.

Chapter Two

PERSONAL AND SOCIAL DEVELOPMENT

A very important area of child development and learning in the early years is an area called 'personal, social and emotional development'. It is concerned with such things as: self-confidence; sociability; 'good' behaviour; popularity; respect for others; sensitivity towards others; independence; self-control; honesty; reliability; cleanliness, practice of good hygiene; sensible eating. . . the list could be never-ending really.

This important area focuses on all of those abstract matters which go towards building a child's personality and the way the child relates to other people in the family, in friendship groups, in the wider community.

The way a child develops as an individual and as a member of different groups such as the family, friends or community, affects a child's ability to learn. Happiness, security, good relationships and a feeling of well-being are vital aspects for their personal, social and emotional development.

THE NEW BABY

Babies know more or less nothing when they're born. They're suddenly plunged into an alien world that totally surrounds them. They have a few reflexes and instincts. Apart from those, from the moment they're born, they're on a quest to make some sort of sense of the world. The psychologist Piaget called this the child's effort to 'construct his own reality', and you can see why. From everything that happens to them, children have to try to work out what the world is all about, and how it fits around them or how they fit into it.

EGOCENTRICITY

To begin with, of course, they think, feel or have an awareness that they are the centre of the world, that everything that surrounds them is linked to them in some way, or is for their benefit. They are, in essence, writing their own scripts for this life drama they've joined. It takes quite a bit of time for them to realise that they're not the only ones with scripts, that everyone else they come into contact with has one too! Gradually, with help from you, they begin to understand that others have needs and feelings as well as them.

THE ROLE OF THE HOME IN DEVELOPMENT

First and foremost, children learn how to relate to others and how they should regard them, from whatever they experience within their homes. That experience can never be changed and, in the formative years, is a considerable factor in defining the children's responses for the rest of their lives.

Take two extremes for an example – if children learn, by their experiences, that home is a friendly, safe, cosy place where everyone is trusted, respected, and treated on equal terms, they are likely to absorb a measure of emotional security that'll stay with them for ever.

If, on the other hand, they learn by experience that home means shouting, bullying, outbreaks of violence, everyone treading on eggshells for fear of upsetting the dominant character in the home, they are more likely to learn to feel insecure, to mistrust others, and either to become a victim or start bullying themselves.

THE INFLUENCE OF PARENTS ON DEVELOPMENT

Children quickly learn to adapt to the attitudes of their parents and, because those parents are their role models, they often *learn* the parents' behaviour and take it on as their own in later years. This is why abused or bullied children become abusers or bullies; they simply accept that it is the way for adults in the home to behave. Studies have shown that it doesn't matter how bad parents are, most very young children still 'look up' to them and love them, simply because they are the security (they may be predictable in their unpredictability) that they know.

DOING OUR BEST

In reality, of course, the majority of our homes are not like that at all. The majority of us simply want to do our best for our children – no matter what that best is – and all of us, in attempting this, sometimes make mistakes, get it wrong in some way or ways. There aren't many parents who, at some stage during their children's lives, aren't compelled to utter those immortal words, 'Where did we go wrong?' – but most of the time, the parents didn't go wrong at all. They were simply misguided, misinformed, or maybe they misjudged the mood of the moment! There is no point wallowing in guilt when things do go wrong because, while you're standing still, wondering how on earth to put things right, your children will be moving onwards, making their own progress, developing in their own ways – and you might as well put the guilt behind you, learn from it and move on with them.

DEVELOPING SELF-AWARENESS

In the early years, children desperately try to define, to themselves, what they are like as unique individuals. They have to try to work out and express the distinctions between themselves and others – particularly between them and their siblings.

You can help them towards self-awareness in very simple ways – use their names when you speak to them, getting them gradually to understand that their name refers only to them. If you have twins, try desperately hard not to refer to them as 'the twins', as this only helps endorse the idea that they are a corporate body.

Encourage the use of pronouns in speech, to help them move from 'me want' towards '*she* gave it to *him*'. Get them to copy actions (for instance, in 'Simon Says'), as this will encourage them to concentrate first on you and then on themselves, and they'll enjoy imitating you.

YOUR CHILD'S SENSE OF SELF

SELF-CONCEPT
As we've already seen, possibly the most important

factor in children's learning is their self-concept. But where do they get that self-concept from?

Of course, it can only grow from how they believe other people see them, most significantly the people who are very important to them – their family or carers, and friends. At this stage of development children, in their immaturity, are particularly vulnerable to the opinions of these people, as they haven't yet learned enough to have formed opinions for themselves.

Therefore, to their mind, what others show they think of them *must* be what they are. It is very important to remember that once they have been assimilated, self-concepts are very, very difficult to alter. You have only to examine some of the beliefs you have about yourself to know that this is true. Suppose, for instance, that at three, you felt you were very shy, and were *treated* as though you were very shy. The chances are that, at thirty-three, you will still feel exactly the same. If, at three, you built the belief that you were stupid or clumsy, it is highly probable that at thirty-three you will indeed display exactly the same behaviour. *Because that is how you learned to believe the world sees you.*

Obviously, then, it's worth really taking time, care and trouble to ensure that your children build themselves positive and realistic self-concepts.

A GOOD SELF-CONCEPT?

Ideal, but realistic, expectations might be for each child: to be confident, without being over-confident; to have self-respect; to have an element of self-control; to have the ability to build effective relationships with other children and adults; to be sensitive to the needs and feelings of others; to be happy to take fair turns; to be willing to share fairly; to be able to express feelings and behave in an appropriate manner and to develop an understanding of right and wrong. You may be able to add other goals to this list.

How to Build Self-esteem

The challenge is to help your children to view themselves positively. This is helped by giving praise, though not indiscriminate praise. If you keep telling them they are wonderful and every single thing that they do is brilliant, they will eventually come to suspect that you have a hidden agenda for saying so, and their self-esteem will immediately take a nosedive.

Help them take pleasure in their small achievements and to understand that they have done well. When you feel that they've displayed or effected one of the goals on your list, for instance in sharing something fairly, say, 'Well done – you were very good at sharing your toys today,' or 'Well done – I'm sure you felt quite shy when you went to the party, but you soon made friends and helped everyone have a good time.' Try to illustrate what you are giving them praise for, so that there's no doubt about the behaviour you're pleased with.

If you have more than one child, try to make regular times for giving each child some individual, undivided attention, and make sure that the others understand and respect this time.

Try to get your child or children to understand that there are times when they get your total, undivided attention and there may be times when they have to share your attention with other people or other

PERSONAL AND SOCIAL DEVELOPMENT

commitments. There has to be flexibility and adaptability, there has to be 'give and take' on both sides.

How to Ensure Feelings of Emotional Security
Children who have good, secure feelings are usually at ease with themselves and others. Of course, situations happen in families that do take away security from children, but in the main, children who are listened to, whose views are taken on board and respected, seem to grow in emotional security, whereas children who are constantly criticised learn to underrate their own abilities and become fearful and hesitant.

If you show your children that you're interested in them, what they are doing or thinking and how they're reacting to the situations around them – whatever those situations are – they'll handle them more confidently and be more emotionally secure. And children who are emotionally secure are better equipped for learning.

Reaching Towards Independence
Children have to be allowed some independence in life or they will remain dependent on others for ever. This means they have to feel free to get things wrong and make mistakes; otherwise, how can they learn what is right? The hardest part is probably for you, in letting them go – but it is only this letting go that will allow them to build the confidence they will need to become a 'separate' person.

Building Confidence
Children need to feel good and positive about themselves before they can mix in a comfortable way with

other children and adults. These good and positive feelings are what give them 'self-confidence'.

You can help to build strong self-confidence by:

• showing an interest and always being supportive when they want to share their experiences and tell you their problems;
• providing lots of different activities for them to tackle and finding one which they are particularly good at, which you can help them to focus on;
• trying not to compare them with others – it's not a lot of help to anyone to be told that they're doing well but their elder brother did even better at their age;
• encouraging self-control so that they make their own choices and decisions, rather than controlling them yourself with strict discipline;
• telling them often that you love them, and like them, and are pleased with them;
• praising their efforts, rather than the outcome of those efforts – rather than concentrating on success or failure, get them to concentrate on their endeavours. A confident child is one who feels 'I did my best' and is happy with that feeling.

HOW TO ENCOURAGE TURN-TAKING

The natural tendency of young children is towards ego-centricity, and it is often very hard for them to realise that they are not actually the centre of the universe. But if you understand that it's because they know so little about the world and have so little experience, that they are constructing the world as it appears to them, you can see why they should feel this way.

One of the first things they have to learn is to 'take turns' and 'share'. Turn-taking comes quite naturally when they are learning to talk. Even a tiny baby will gurgle to you, wait for you to gurgle back, and then gurgle again. They seem to understand the *concept* of taking turns right from their earliest days.

Unfortunately, as they begin to mature, sometimes they find it more difficult to actually apply the skill, particularly where brothers and sisters are concerned! It is difficult for young children to be able to see the world from others' points of view, but this doesn't mean they are 'selfish', it just means that they haven't reached an appropriate stage of maturity yet.

You can encourage the idea of turn-taking in quite simple ways, for example, equip yourself and the child with a toy or junk-model telephone each, and speak, wait for a response, speak, wait for a response. Play games where you naturally take turns, such as a version of tiddlywinks, or board games. Recite nursery rhymes together – you begin, then leave a gap for the child to fill in, and so on.

HOW TO ENCOURAGE INTERACTION

Children usually need the company of other children by the time they're about two years old. They will quickly get bored and irritable, even uncooperative, if they have to play for too long on their own. Of course, this does not mean that two-year-olds can play together happily *ad infinitum* without squabbling – but the squabbling is all part of the learning to interact and socialise.

By the time they're around the age of three they'll be much more sociable and you will see their ability to play with other children get better and better as they grow and mature. Try to show them that their friendships are important to you: have picnics and play sessions to which friends are invited and leave the children as unsupervised as possible to give them chance to build up their social skills for themselves. Try not to intervene unless it's absolutely necessary. If the children simply cannot cooperate on a certain activity, take it away with good humour and replace it with something else. Try not to make a big thing about it.

COPING WITH SHYNESS

Children who display shyness or a tendency to withdraw from social interaction need to be helped to feel secure in new situations and supported in handling them. You can't force shy children to be sociable, but neither can you assume that they will 'grow out of it' without any help.

Try to keep calm when the children are exhibiting their shyness. Don't apologise for their shyness in their hearing, because you will only emphasise, to them, the fact that their shyness is a problem, and you will also be reinforcing the fact that they *have* that problem. It's better to talk about the emotion with the child when you're alone, and say 'We all feel like that sometimes'. This way you are showing that you understand, and you'll make them feel better about themselves.

It's hard for a shy child to cope with meeting lots of new people at once, so try to arrange for activities that involve only small groups to begin with. Although shy children find all kinds of strategies for going off to play alone, encourage them to play in twos or threes and set up games and activities that need others to join in.

Shy children often feel that nobody likes them, or that there's something drastically wrong with them. Reassure them, by letting them know you care for them even when they're displaying shyness, and just say that you're sure they'd have more fun if they joined in with the others.

WHAT ABOUT DISCIPLINE?

Sooner or later the whole question of 'good' behaviour and 'discipline' raises its head. Most people want their children to display good and appropriate behaviour, but are quite at a loss to how they can inculcate this into their children, other than by giving them a set of rules to follow and imposing a form of discipline which involves sanctions and punishments or rewards.

The best word to remember, at all times, is 'positive'. Mostly, the things you do or say that are 'positive' will rub off on your child; most of what you do or say that is negative will not.

This applies to 'rules' as well as everything else. If you say, 'We always put our toys away before we go to bed,' you will have a better chance of achieving success than if you say, 'Don't leave the toys lying about.'

TOWARDS SELF-CONTROL

Discipline that's asserted from outside the children is not a lot of good to anyone. It might fulfil short-term aims but it won't get you far in the long run. Far better for the children to develop a form of self-control that comes from within them – not from the knowledge that they'll be punished or rewarded for it, but from the feeling that it is a respectful and sensitive way to behave towards others. Of course, everybody finds it difficult to manage their children sometimes, but giving in for the sake of peace, or administering a smack out of frustration are patently not the most expedient ways of fostering their self-control.

'Giving in' only teaches children that if they make enough noise and enough fuss they will be able to get their own way. They *learn* the kind of behaviour that gets them what they want.

Smacking is usually the result of the perpetrator's frustration and temper, and often carries with it negative feelings and guilt for doing it. Often its greatest effect is to inflame the situation. Smackers often do something to 'spoil' the children after the smack to alleviate their own bad feelings, so what was the point of it in the beginning? The children *learn* a cycle of bad, good, bad, good, but they do not learn how to control their own behaviour.

WHY CONSISTENCY MATTERS

The main thing is to be consistent, both in your 'rules' or expectations, and in your methods of dealing with problems. If you have to say 'no' and it provokes a temper tantrum, try to remain calm, and take the child out of the situation. If you find yourself losing your temper, walk away if at all possible. Try to get a break from the situation for a couple of minutes, while you calm down. Consistent treatment shows children where the lines are drawn as your responses are not unpredictable.

If you're in a situation where you can't walk away, such as a supermarket, take a deep breath and try not to let the situation assume enormous proportions inside your head. Hold the child firmly, say 'No' in a calm but firm way, and mean it. Remember, the calmer you appear, the more likely the child is to respond.

Once a child has reached the state of being 'out of control', she or he may be totally unable to get out of the emotional situation for her or himself and, often, the child is very afraid of the feeling of being out of control. Try to stay calm and relaxed – even if you don't feel it, act as if you do! A cuddle often helps because, even though the child shrinks away, he or she can be reassured by caring physical contact. Quietly reassure the child that there's no point in getting so upset, everything will be fine in the end, but state, quietly and firmly (and mean it for yourself as well!), that this kind of behaviour won't result in you giving in. Get out of the place you're in and move to somewhere else as soon as you can, because relocating will help to take some of the sting out of the tantrum.

Another tactic is to try distraction techniques. Try to ignore the temper and carry on chatting to the child as though nothing's happening; perhaps bring up a different topic of conversation or interest him or her in a favourite toy.

Whatever happens, try not to let your own embarrassment or tension make you respond in an angry way, because it really doesn't help. On the whole, your calmness in any temper situation will help the child become less agitated. Once she or he sees that you have remained relaxed, the child will begin, eventually, to quieten down. Easier said than done, obviously, but if you can keep repeating to yourself, in your mind, that you are remaining calm for the child's sake, you can teach yourself to do it!

Try to elicit some compromise between all the members of your household so that each knows and has a measure of agreement on how your 'discipline' measures will work. It's very important that your treatment of the child is seen (through his or her eyes) to be both consistent and fair. If they think they can 'get away with it' by playing one member of the family off against another, they will soon bring you to chaos. Explain to them, together, that bad behaviour will not bring the results they want – and make sure you mean it. Let them know that you expect them, as they're growing up and getting more mature, to discuss things with you, rather than losing their temper.

If they do not respond, you just have to keep on being firm, being calmly assertive, and reiterating that when you say 'No' (or whatever) you mean it. Eventually, most children realise when they are up against a brick wall, and resort to different tactics. But remember, the earlier you begin to prepare them for self-control, the less likely you are to reach this point.

HOW MUCH SELF-CONTROL CAN YOU REALISTICALLY EXPECT?

Much will depend upon the child's level of emotional maturity, of course, but try to bear in mind that:

• a baby cannot possibly be expected to understand any 'rules' or expectations and probably, when you worry about whether your crying child should be picked up or left, you should really follow your heart and your instincts, rather than your desire to instil 'discipline';

• between about nine months and one year, children begin to understand the meanings of 'yes' and 'no' – they also perceive your approval or your disapproval, but this doesn't mean that they will always do what you want them to do!;

• by the time they're about eighteen months, they can be very wilful and often confrontational – although it's frustrating, it is totally normal behaviour!;

• the 'terrible twos' are known for increasing determination and temper in toddlers. Two-year-olds have yet to learn patience – they act impulsively, without any consideration for others;

• by three, children have usually begun to appreciate that *everyone* (not just them!) has to live according to certain expectations and, though you might expect them to rebel against this, it usually gives them an added sense of security;

• by four, they will expect you to be fair, and not to break the rules yourself. They will also have no compunction in telling off others for behaving badly. By now, they will also have learned to feel 'sorry' when they have done something wrong;

• hopefully, by five, children will have learned enough about rules and control to not need you to tell them, all the time, how to behave.

LEARNING WHAT'S RIGHT AND WRONG

Psychologists agree that the understanding of 'right and wrong' develops in stages, and much depends upon the child's level of maturity.

Most children will 'tell lies' at some point, but their reasons for lying may vary from distorted memory, through self-deception, to a blurred line between fantasy and reality. Be calm, consistent and positive. Say, 'This is what really happened,' and encourage them to deal with the consequences of their behaviour. For example, if they have blamed someone else for something they have done, help them to apologise. If they have denied something that you know they have done – spilt the paint or whatever – insist that they clear up the mess with you.

The same goes for stealing. A child can only really 'steal' when the concept of 'personal possession' is fully understood. Until then, stealing may be a form of 'borrowing' or 'sharing', or something challenging and exciting to do. Show your disapproval in a calm way, and point out the consequences of the action. Help them give the stolen item back and to apologise. Make sure the child really feels your disapproval of the action and knows that it's not an acceptable form of behaviour.

Swearing is something most children pick up at some point in their early years. The younger they are, the more tempted you may be to laugh, but this only encourages them. Tell them, quite firmly, that swearing is not a pleasant thing to do and that you disapprove of the words they have used. Explain that if other people hear them using swear words they will think badly of them. Tell them that no matter who they have over-heard using the bad words, it doesn't matter, they are not good words for anyone to use – children especially – and that you really do not like it.

BAD TIMES

It would be something of a miracle if all early periods of development went by without some 'bad times' occurring. These may include illness or hospitalisation; separation from known and loved-ones or the death of someone loved. Young children often find these events totally bewildering and traumatic; it is as though the ground has been taken away from under their feet.

At these times, they need lots of loving care and reassurance so that the trauma doesn't have a negative long-term effect on them. It's very important to give lots of opportunity and encouragement to get their feelings out into the open and talk about them. Help them by talking about your own feelings. Reassure them that sadness, pain and grief don't last for ever, and although bad times are hard to get through, you have each other and your mutual love will help you both. Be as honest as you can so that they don't get the feeling you're hiding anything from them; such feelings lead to distrust and insecurity and now, more than ever, they need to feel that they can rely upon you totally.

Search the bookshops and libraries for books and stories about comparable situations. Use them to help your children understand their strong emotions and work through difficult situations.

PRACTICAL ACTIVITIES

You can give positive help towards your children's personal, social and emotional development by:

• giving praise and physical affection when possible;

- listening to worries and concerns and discussing them in a respectful way;
- taking time to talk about happenings, ideas, thoughts and feelings;
- talking through mistakes or things that have gone wrong in a sensible way, and getting them to understand that a mistake is not the end of the world, and to respond accordingly;
- encouraging them to practise self-discipline;
- encouraging them to make choices and decisions about daily events and routines;
- enabling them to solve problems for themselves;
- showing them the consequences of their actions;
- concentrating on positive, affirmative behaviour rather than constantly criticising negative behaviour;
- using stories to help them understand sadness and pleasure, illness and loss;
- playing board games together; inviting other children to play and encouraging return visits;
- giving them individual responsibilities such as their own bit of garden to grow and look after, helping with shopping, looking after pets;
- demonstrating how to treat possessions, people and places with care and concern;
- teaching them how to wash and dress themselves;
- encouraging 'dressing-up' activities, where they can pretend to be other people and look at life from a different perspective;
- helping them to reassure and comfort other children during their 'bad' times;
- remembering that you are always your child's first role model.

Chapter Three

DEVELOPING LANGUAGE ABILITY

NEVER TOO SOON TO LEARN

Right from the moment you cradle your new baby in your arms and begin to whisper to him or her, you are actually teaching the child language. It's never too soon to begin to develop your child's abilities in language and you are always, always the child's first teacher.

Most children are born with all the faculties they will need to enable them to learn to talk. They have adequate vision, hearing, intelligence and motor skills. The skills children are born with are allowed to develop with the help of the world around them.

LEARNING 'ENGLISH'
In education today, particularly in the early and primary school years, we talk of 'language development' and 'literacy development' rather than 'learning English'.

WHAT IS LANGUAGE AND LITERACY DEVELOPMENT?

By 'language', basically we mean talking and listening. Children need to develop :

- listening skills: this is more than 'hearing', it is listening attentively, understanding, interpreting and forming a response;
- receptive language: this is 'understanding'. Children hear or listen – in other words, they 'receive' language and they understand its meaning. Even from babyhood children understand much more than they can say;
- expressive language: this is the ability to talk in order to express themselves – to use words, phrases, sentences – to make intelligible conversation.

By 'literacy' we mean reading and writing.

THE IMPORTANCE OF LANGUAGE AND LITERACY DEVELOPMENT

Language development is very important for two reasons: first, the fact that most children learn to speak their home language quite naturally within the first four years of their lives shows you that they have a good capacity to learn. Second, once they begin school or a pre-school group like nursery or playschool, speaking and listening become the principal means of their learning in all other areas.

When they start more formal schooling, they will be taught to read and write, and their abilities in reading and writing will make all the difference to how much they learn in all other areas of the school curriculum. They will need to be able to read textbooks, worksheets, notes from the teacher . . . all manner of reading material. And they will need to be able to write their own explanations, stories, reference material, projects etc, in order to demonstrate what they have learned.

LANGUAGE AND LITERACY GO TOGETHER

You can see from this that literacy plays a huge part in the school life of any child. And, obviously, literacy begins with language – if children have no language ability whatsoever, how on earth do you teach them to read and write? If they don't know what words mean, or cannot say them, how can they interpret them from squiggles on pages? The more children have already learned at home, as a matter of course, the greater their foundation will be for the formal learning they are about to meet in school, and the easier it'll be for them.

HOW CHILDREN LEARN TO SPEAK AND LISTEN

There are several theories to explain how children learn language but, of course, none of them can be proved, though some are more plausible than others.

LANGUAGE BY IMITATION

The theory that's been held the longest is that children acquire language simply by imitation. It asserts that children reflect the words and sounds that they hear around them. While this may be true in the early stages of language acquisition, it doesn't explain how, say, a three-year-old can make up a complex sentence that he/she's never heard before. The imitation theory ignores the fact that children somehow absorb the grammatical structure of their home language and learn how to manipulate words and meanings.

LANGUAGE BY REINFORCEMENT

There is the theory that language is acquired because

41

the adults who surround the child reinforce certain words and phrases constantly, so that the child, hearing the same things repeatedly, is encouraged to use them. In this theory, children learn vocabulary because it is constantly repeated and because they associate the words with their context – for instance, they learn what 'garden' means when you repeatedly say, 'Let's play in the garden,'; but it doesn't really explain why or how children learn more intangible concepts – for instance, how do they learn what an 'idea' is?

LANGUAGE AS AN EXTENSION OF 'GROWING'

Another theory is that children are born with the ability to speak and use language and that they can distinguish language from other sounds and noises in the environment. Given that the majority of children progress through the same stages, in the same order, at approximately the same chronological time in their lives, it could be assumed that learning language is a natural process of growing, and it develops in much the same way as the child's physical body develops.

LANGUAGE BY INTERACTION

A further theory, one that most educationists seem to uphold at the time of writing this book, is that language develops by interaction between children's innate ability to communicate and stimuli from their environment. The children experience a constant cycle of action-reaction-action and, through this cycle, develop their speech and language skills. This theory seems to be borne out by the fact that when children enter playgroup, nursery or school, it is easy to discern or assess, from their ability to manipulate language or understand, what their language experience has been so far.

BILINGUAL CHILDREN

It's interesting to note that children who hear two languages from a very early age – imagine a mother speaks one and the father another; perhaps they speak each other's languages to each other and to the child – usually grow up able to operate in both languages competently and confidently, without any problems. Usually they can switch from one language to another at the drop of a hat, and usually they understand – without being told – which language to use with different members of the family.

Their knowledge and understanding actually tells us a lot about how language works and is learned. Without having formal lessons, these children learn the grammatical structures of each language, as well as the vocabulary. They seem to *absorb* each language as a separate entity, and completely understand that the two are not mixed together. This kind of 'immersion' process really points towards the theory of the constant cycle of action-reaction-action.

IMPORTANCE OF HEARING A LANGUAGE

It doesn't matter which theory or theories you think may be right. You are at liberty to take any of those theories and try to apply them to how your child is learning language, and see which one seems to fit their learning most comfortably. One thing is certain and absolute: if children do not *hear* language, there is no way they will be able to *learn* language. There's a well-known myth about a boy who grew up in the chicken shed and could only make chicken noises. Think how difficult it is for a child with hearing-impaired parents – without outside support, the child finds it increasingly difficult to communicate in spoken language.

LISTEN TO YOURSELF

You can help your children develop their skills by talking to them and giving them the opportunity to listen and to talk for themselves. They'll be listening to *what* you say and *how* you say it. Pay attention to your own voice – try to listen to yourself. Try to engage them in eye contact – if they're looking at you they're usually listening to you. Aim at speaking clearly, with good intonation and appropriate volume. You don't need to shout at children to make them listen – in fact, shouting actually causes them *not* to listen! Any primary school teacher will tell you that if, in a noisy classroom, you lower your voice and whisper to someone, the room will become silent, as if by magic, and the children will become 'all ears'!

Use simple explanations – if you go off at a tangent or become clumsy in explaining something, children lose the thread and stop listening. If you *listen* to yourself and analyse the way you speak to your children, you are halfway towards getting *them* to listen to *you*.

ROLE-MODELLING

There is probably no better demonstration of role-modelling than in the case of language and literacy development. If your children, from the beginning, hear you talking, see you reading and writing – and enjoying using all those skills – they will want to do the same and will find it perfectly natural that they should.

Imagine a child growing up in a home where everybody talks to everybody else, where there's lots of discussion going on all the time, where books and reading are part of the everyday pattern, where writing – letters, notes, whatever – has an important slot in home life. And then think of the opposite – a child growing up in a home where people only speak when they have to, where the family never have discussions over meals, where children are told to be 'seen and not heard', where books or magazines are things that have to be tidied away, where no one ever writes to anyone for any reason. Which child do you think will have the better communication skills?

WHEN CHILDREN WON'T HEAR A LANGUAGE

Listening is very much the children's key into language, so you want to make it something that they do as a normal action or response. This won't happen if:

- there's always noise in the house, with television or radio on constantly, particularly if it's at high volume;
- everybody talks to everybody else all the time, and nobody listens to anyone;
- people feel they have to raise their voice to have any effect in a conversation.

Children who grow up in this kind of atmosphere often find it impossible to pay more than a few seconds' attention to anything. Parents learn to dismiss this trait with 'Oh, they don't listen to anything,' and it seems to be a perfectly acceptable way to behave. By the time they reach school they have learned to 'not listen', and they can 'switch off' at will. This ability causes tremendous difficulties in the classroom.

HOW TO GET CHILDREN TO LISTEN
The way to teach children to listen is to:

- eliminate background noise as much as is possible;
- make sure that people look at each other and engage in eye contact when they are talking;
- get the children sometimes to repeat or corroborate what you have been saying to them;
- play games like 'We went shopping and we bought . . .'. You do this in turns: the first person says an item; the next person says that item and another one; the third person says the first two items and a third, and so on, until you have so many items that everybody has difficulty in remembering. There are many variations of this game, which you can play with just two people. It's also something you can play in the car on long journeys, and is particularly good for developing memory and recall skills, and for making children listen.

WHAT YOU AS A PARENT CAN DO

TALK TO BABIES FROM BIRTH
It can't be emphasised enough that the ideal is to talk to babies right from birth, giving them lots of space and opportunity to 'talk' back to you. Sometimes you hear people saying, 'What's the point of talking to a baby? It can't understand what you say!', but how will it ever

understand if it doesn't hear and absorb the rhythms, patterns and meanings of speech?

USE NURSERY RHYMES

Nursery rhymes are good for all kinds of reasons, not least because babies get used to the repetitions and the melodies. If you sing nursery rhymes to babies you'll see that they soon begin to look you in the eye while they are listening. Establish eye contact with them and sing or recite one rhyme repeatedly. It won't be long before they begin to respond right from the start of the rhyme. They recognise, from your tone of voice and your facial expression, as well as from the words, something enjoyable, something familiar, and they want to join in.

As they get older, they begin to join in, making appropriate sounds, even if they don't say the actual words, and using intonation in the same way you do.

While they're learning the sounds of the nursery rhymes, they're also beginning to develop their literacy skills – strange as it may seem! You may not be showing them the words or pointing out the pictures on the pages, but they are definitely learning that some things can be told over and over again and that these things retain their meaning, their sounds and their rhythms, – they do not change. Eventually, when they see those very same nursery rhymes written and illustrated on the pages of books, they will love the books because they are familiar. They will understand this quality of 'sameness' and this will then help them to learn to read.

SHOW THEM THE PRINTED WORD

They will be able to sing the rhymes and follow the

printed words at the same time. This step of 'reading from memory' is the first step to learning to read. You may hear people dismiss this as nonsense – 'They're not *reading*, they're just *remembering*,' – but that's exactly one of the ways we learn to read. We learn that the squiggles on the page remain unchanged and say the same thing time after time. We learn to decipher the squiggles. This is what the children do when they learn to follow familiar rhymes in their books.

INVOLVE THEM IN BOOKS
Just as it's never too early to begin talking with your child, it's never too early to involve them with books.

Even tiny babies enjoy the movement of the pages turning and the sound of the paper. They will experience lots of pleasure from lying in your arms, listening to the sound of your voice.

In the beginning, babies can only discriminate colours, shapes and patterns on the pages, but as their ability to discriminate visually matures, they'll start to recognise shapes and begin to associate those shapes with the sounds you make when you point to them.

They will then progress to turning pages for themselves and making their own sounds to tell you what's happening on the pages. Finally, they'll begin to follow the sequence of the stories and pictures and be able to connect the words with these sequences. They will learn to put the words to the pictures on the pages; they will learn to recognise the squiggles that are the words.

WHAT THEY ARE LEARNING
More than anything else, at this very early point, babies

are learning that sharing books is a pleasurable, comfortable and rewarding activity. Usually, once learned, this feeling or attitude will stay with them for ever. You might consider that you have *conditioned* them to enjoy books. This will give them tremendous motivation for learning to read which, hopefully, they will never lose.

They are learning other things at the same time: to develop their ability to concentrate and to be attentive. They are developing their powers of understanding, as they encounter tales, poems and stories which take them into new realms of life. They are learning to appreciate how other people feel and how they cope with problems. They're developing their imagination and enlarging their knowledge of what happens in the world.

ENCOURAGE THEM TO WRITE

As with reading, so with writing. Show, by example, that writing is an important and enjoyable activity in your life. Let your children, from the earliest days, see that it's natural for you to communicate by writing.

As soon as your children can hold a crayon, encourage them to scribble away to their heart's content. Ask them what their 'stories' say. Encourage them to read them back to you, showing that you respect what they have 'written' and that it is as important as what you write yourself. Make up stories together and write the words on the pages for them. Get them to 'write' too. At this stage you should pay no attention to whether the squiggles are real letters or words – they're learning that there is a strong relationship between talking, reading and writing. They will come, in time, to understand that the squiggles have to be of a certain kind.

By the time they are about four, they will probably be able to write their own name and have a stab at other letters and words that are familiar – for example, 'Love from' on greetings cards, 'Dear Grandad' on letters, 'Teddy' and others. Help them to build up their own collection of vocabulary for writing.

ENCOURAGE YOUR CHILD TO USE WHOLE WORDS

Many children learn to read and write a healthy bank of whole words before they learn to break them down into letters or bits of words. Encourage this facility, as it will give your child lots of confidence, but remember that it isn't a complete method for teaching reading or writing, because eventually the ability to memorise more and more whole words reaches saturation point.

LANGUAGE AND GENDER

Sometimes it is harder to interest boys in language activities than girls. Again, it's debated whether this is more to do with the way female and male brains develop, or innate traits and inclinations. However, if it happens to you, try not to be put off or to assume your boys are 'failing' in any way. If they're hard to motivate before attending school, and you give up, they'll be even harder to motivate when they get to school!

Try to ensure that you pick subjects and topics that interest them. Boys are notoriously keen to explore and to learn about 'facts', so, for example, when you're choosing books for them, look out for books on the kinds of things that they like rather than sticking to story or poetry books. It doesn't matter what 'vehicle' you use for encouraging language, as long as the language is encouraged!

Remember that reading isn't just about books. Children are reading when they are looking at the instructions for games, when they're scanning comics, looking at road signs, reading the blurb about the give-away on the cornflakes box, and so on. Just try, in any ways that you can, to interest them in the written word.

PRACTICAL ACTIVITIES

For listening:
• use an interesting, tuneful voice, with lots of intonation; vary your volume and the speed at which you speak;
• talk to the children while you do things together;
• wait for your children to respond, then respond back and leave a space for them to come back yet again;
• play the listening game: close your eyes, keep very still and quiet. How many sounds can they hear? What are they?;
• with your children, tape-record different sounds around the house and garden. Play the sounds back and see if they can recognise them;
• play 'Whispers': whisper instructions and see whether they can carry them out. Start with one instruction, then give two, then give three, etc;
• make different instruments from household articles – washing-up liquid bottles with rice, pebbles, paper clips, sugar. Shake the containers and listen to the different sounds. Make two the same and see whether they can identify them;

- tell familiar nursery rhymes and stories – miss bits out and if they're listening, they will challenge you.

For talking:
- encourage early use of a cup (without a spout), a straw, and the eating of food with different chewing textures. This will help to develop the muscles that are necessary for speech;
- make a scrapbook of family and friends, including pets and toys, and ask what/who the pictures show;
- encourage the children to help you with household chores – sorting the washing etc, and talk through the activity: 'This is Debbie's dress, Daddy's blue shirt,' etc;
- have garden or living-room 'picnics' for Teddy and other toys – with the child talking for the toys;
- encourage them to tell you what certain objects are for: 'We use the hairdrier to dry our hair after we've washed it', 'We go to Nanny's house in the car,' etc;
- encourage role-play, for example, washing toy cars or dressing toys with the children pretending to be you and talking through their activities;
- play dressing-up games – use shoes, accessories, hats etc, and pretend to be other people. All role-play encourages language development;
- play variations of 'Simon Says' to teach the vocabulary for different body parts, for example, 'Simon says touch your knees, Simon says lie on your tummy,' etc;
- share and provide as rich a range of experiences as you can; for children to talk, they need something to talk about.

For reading:
- familiarise them with their own names, written on badges, birthday cards, paintings;
- read aloud together, regularly (ten minutes every day is much better than an hour once in a blue moon). Make this sharing time special and cosy;
- choose books with colourful pictures and few words to begin with. Make sure the content is of interest to the children. Talk about the pictures; ask the children to point out and name what they can see;
- show, by example, how the book opens and the pages turn; occasionally run your finger, slowly and continuously, along the words as they go from left to right, to show them the direction the words work in;
- pick out key words in a story and show them to the children;
- encourage them to say the story through with you, or to recount the story to you in their own words;
- give plenty of time for the children to look at the pictures and decide what's happening in the story;
- give lots of praise;
- keep sessions short so that they don't get bored;

For writing:
- provide lots of activities like bead-threading which will develop hand–eye co-ordination;
- encourage imaginative games and pretend-play to develop the children's imagination;
- provide paint-brushes, crayons and chalks to give them the idea of mark-making;
- do printing activities, using paint and bits and pieces like leaves, cotton reels etc, which will show

the children how to make the same mark repeatedly;
- use magnetic plastic letters (make sure they're not all capital letters) to write the children's names on the fridge and, perhaps, make messages;
- when they start to learn letters, provide Plasticene or play-dough to roll letters out with;
- make your own books, using family photographs etc. Get the children to decide what they want the words to say, write the words clearly in black, and read them back, often, together.

Chapter Four

DEVELOPING MATHEMATICS SKILLS

When you hear the word 'mathematics', more than likely you'll think of arithmetic – numbers – and, even more likely still, probably the four rules of numbers (addition, subtraction, multiplication, division). But mathematics is really about much more than numbers.

In a way our whole lives revolve around mathematics, or mathematics revolves around us. You don't have to think for very long to realise the things you do in ordinary daily events that use maths. For instance, you might:

- cook something, or make a sandwich or salad for the family;
- do enough shopping to keep the family going for a week or a month;
- budget for something and check your bank statement;
- read a timetable and work out a route;
- follow a map;
- plan an outing or a holiday;
- knit a stuffed toy, make a dress from a pattern or a wooden toy from a model;
- count the money in your pocket;

- play a card or board-game;
- decorate a room or tile a kitchen;
- check the time and work out how long you've got before your meeting.

All of these things involve maths skills in some way. In fact, once you try to work out just how many of your activities *do* use maths skills of one sort or another you'll probably be amazed at the amount of maths you cover in any one day. Rather than being just about numbers or arithmetic, maths is about shape and space, or *spatial awareness*, about measurement and about using and applying mathematical knowledge for solving problems.

Children need lots of play experience with numbers, spatial awareness, measurement and problem-solving to help them become efficient at maths. They use maths in the same way as you, probably without either of you being aware of it. And it begins very, very early in their lives.

Maths in a typical day for children involves them in:

- waking up and finding out it's morning – just by doing this they are being acquainted with the measurement of time and making a deduction;
- getting dressed – this involves them with sorting and matching, and making decisions;
- having breakfast – if they pour out cornflakes they're estimating how much they might eat, how much will fill the bowl, how much milk the cornflakes need;
- going shopping – they're learning about direction

and numbers: 'How many tins of beans will we buy?' and probably weighing: 'Let's weigh the apples before we put them in the trolley,';
• putting the shopping away – sorting the shopping into things that go in the fridge or the cupboard, etc, categorising items into different sets (fruit, vegetables, meat etc), fitting things together;
• playing with toys, making mud pies etc – experimenting all the time with shape, size, weight etc;
• going for a walk to the park – again time, direction, distance;
• having tea – laying the table helps with planning, sorting, matching and counting skills;
• putting toys away – sorting, matching, categorising;
• having a bath – playing in the bath (pouring, tipping and splashing) is experimenting with volume;
• bedtime – time and sequence.

During all these activities the children are learning, in an informal way, how maths functions in everyday life.

ABOUT NUMERACY – COUNTING

Once they begin to get used to the sound of numbers, children are eager to learn to count. Counting is the basis for all number work and it's something they really need to learn to do, but there's a bit more to it than just learning to say the numbers in their correct order.

PRACTISING COUNTING

You can practise counting very easily, right from baby-hood. As you're dressing the baby you can be saying,

'Let's put one arm in, let's put two arms in,' etc. You can say, 'We need four carrots for tea – let's count four out.' You can do 'three cheers' and 'how many piggies?' etc, count how many birds come to the garden, how many legs the dog has, etc, and there are innumerable number rhymes that you can sing with your children.

ONE-TO-ONE CORRESPONDENCE – ONE NUMBER FOR ONE OBJECT

When the children learn to recite the numbers in the correct order, what they are really doing is learning the *names* of numbers. What they also have to learn is that, as they count, one number is for each object, without missing any out or counting any more than once. In other words, to count to five they need to have five objects, and to touch each one in turn as they say *one, two, three, four, five*. There's a special term for the ability to relate one number to one object – it is called *one-to-one correspondence* and it's an important basic concept.

Teachers test for one-to-one correspondence by asking children to do things like set out a cup for each of a group of teddies. If the children can relate how many teddies there are to how many cups they need, they have more than likely assimilated the difficult concept.

One-to-one correspondence is not something you can compel a child to know, it has to come to them through frequent repetition, through constantly doing 'Let's count the stairs as we climb them; Let's lay the table – how many places do we need? How many spoons? How many forks?; Let's count the apples in the bowl,' etc. Eventually, through constant repetition, children come to understand that if they miss any objects out, or if they count any of them more than once, the numbers will be wrong.

CONSERVATION OF NUMBER – THE NUMBER OF THINGS REMAINS UNALTERED

Eventually children learn that the number of things in a group doesn't alter even if you move them around or count them in a different order. At this point they are said to understand *conservation of number*.

An example of this is: suppose you have five toy cars arranged in a bunch, the child counts them and gets five. Suppose you then rearrange the cars so that they are nose to tail in a long line and ask the child, 'How many cars are there now?' A child who hasn't arrived at the point of conservation will look at the line of cars, think it is longer or bigger than the bunch and therefore assume there could be more. You then have to get the child to count again, touching with the finger, to get her or him to appreciate that there are still five.

Try another experiment. Take the same set of cars and put them side by side in a totally different order and ask the question, 'How many cars are there now?' What happens if you begin counting the cars from the third car (as car one) instead of at the beginning of the row – do they think the numbers will be different?

Sometimes children who have a good feel or awareness of numbers can look at a group of, say, three, and tell you there are three without counting them. This is a completely different perceptual skill, something akin to recognising 'whole words' in reading. Getting them to break down the set or group into single units and count them sometimes results in the children losing the skill altogether. So, if your child can do it, and is always right, encourage it.

MORE THAN, LESS THAN, THE SAME

One of the next important things to learn about numbers is how they change when you put more objects in or take some away. They need to develop the concepts of *more than, less than* and *the same*.

'The same' is sometimes quite difficult because the child may get confused. You need to spell out the fact that you are talking about numbers of things, not about whether they're the same or different to look at, to hold etc. In order to prevent this kind of confusion the child should have had lots of practice in *sorting and matching*.

SORTING AND MATCHING

Any activity that involves sorting and matching, comparing, or putting things in some sort of order, is valuable to the mathematics learning of growing children because it helps them to form some basis for logic, for decision-making and for problem-solving.

Sorting into groups is an essential part of the learning-to-count process. For instance, sorting fruit into sets or groups of oranges, apples and bananas and then counting each set will help children to learn and appreciate sameness and difference and understand how categories work. While they're sorting out the oranges they are matching them, while they're sorting out the bananas they're matching them – *this object is the same as this object, but it is different from the others*.

They are also learning lots of maths language, and that while different things may belong to one *whole* group (fruit), they can also be sorted into smaller groups where they must have certain properties that are the same.

All of these skills are important to understanding how numbers, and the patterns in numbers, work.

THE SYMBOLS

Possibly the last part of the counting activity is actually learning what the numbers look like – 1, 2, 3, 4, 5.

Don't try to teach your child too many numbers at once – 1, 2 and 3 are fine for three-year-olds.

Probably the easiest way to introduce the symbols for numbers is on birthday cards. The number for their own age is usually the number they have most feeling for; it holds some meaning for children, almost like their name. Make a big thing of having the right number of candles on the cake. Write the birthday number on the card or make a badge – whatever. They will soon begin to recognise 'their' number. They'll also like to look out for the numbers that belong to their brothers and sisters or for the numbers that belong to your house or car.

While they are learning these symbols, don't give up the counting practice. This is important because they eventually need to get to understand the link between the one, two, three, four, five cars that they can count and figure 5.

WRITING NUMBERS
If children show an interest in writing the numbers as soon as they can recognise them, help them write them in the conventional way, making sure they begin at the

right place and move their crayon in the right direction (*see below*). Don't be upset if they write them the wrong way round at first (young children often reverse some letters and numbers), but help them do it the right way round, calmly and with lots of patience. The more often they do it wrong, the less it looks 'wrong' to them and the harder it becomes to change their way of writing.

Start at the dot, follow the arrows

SPATIAL AWARENESS

Spatial awareness is the knowledge you have that enables you to:

• estimate how much seed or turf you'll need for a patch on your lawn;
• estimate how far away each place setting can be to fit eight round the table;
• estimate whether a pair of shorts will fit your child;
• estimate whether or not you'll be able to get all the shopping in the freezer;

- recognise that a circle is two-dimensional and a sphere is three-dimensional;
- work out how you can rearrange the furniture;
- work out whether or not you can get your car into a parking space.

Children develop spatial awareness gradually, through their experiences of exploring space.

When they first start to roll and crawl and toddle, they are exploring space. Climbing, jumping, swinging, sliding and dancing are also all ways of exploring space. They are exploring space and shape when they are curling themselves into small shapes, or stretching themselves as long or as tall as they can be. They are exploring space when they are hiding in a cupboard or behind the sofa, and when they're walking in a wiggly path along the street.

By increasing their knowledge of their own bodies, children learn different ways of moving in space, and of fitting into shape and space. They are learning all about *far* and *near*, about *close* and *a long way away*.

FITTING THINGS TOGETHER

Eventually, the children's awareness leads them into positions where they can *fit things together*. For instance, they learn how to do puzzles – the little wooden inset puzzles with shaped pictures where they take out the pictures and have to get them back into the right-shaped hole help them to understand some of the connection between space and shape, as well as developing hand–eye co-ordination and fine motor control. Jigsaw puzzles help them to observe and distinguish shapes and spaces, and put them together in a logical way. They usually begin with puzzles that have only three or four pieces that fit together as outlines, and move on to much more complex puzzles where the shapes of the pieces have little or no connection to the part of the picture that's on them.

Don't push your children to do more than they are capable of. Break any task down into small stages and give lots of help – remember this is a *learning* situation, not a *test* of ability. Sometimes children find it quite difficult to actually begin a jigsaw or shape puzzle. If you help with the first couple of pieces it gives them a better idea of how the puzzle works.

Playing with toy farms/dolls' houses, with toy food preparation or toy garages all help to develop spatial awareness: 'Can the farmer get all the cows in the field?' 'Which plates do we need for the sandwiches – the little ones or the big ones?' 'How many cars will fit into the lift?' The children's imagination will provide the focus for the play – your careful intervention can provide the impetus for learning.

MEASUREMENT

At this level we're not talking about measuring things with a rule or tape measure to get an accurate assessment of size. What we're looking at is more a method of comparison. Is something:

- bigger or smaller than something else?
- fatter or thinner than something else?
- wider or narrower than something else?

- taller or shorter than something else?
- longer or shorter than something else?
- heavier or lighter than something else?
- emptier or fuller than something else?
- enough, not enough, or too much?

and so on.

We have lots of different ways of 'measuring' things. For instance, we may say that a spider in the bath is 'enormous' but if we compare it with an elephant we can see that it's nothing of the kind! Lots of this kind of comparison will give children a 'feeling' for size.

HOW CHILDREN MEASURE

In the natural way of things children, who're making sense of the world, may sound quite confused about measurement but, of course, their thinking is quite logical for the stage of development they are at.

For instance, children may think that someone who is taller than someone else is older. They may think that a big, splashy picture takes longer to paint than a small, detailed one, just because it is bigger. They think that a tall, narrow jug holds much more water than a short, fat one – because the water level is higher. They may think that days are not the same length of time at all – the day Grandma comes is much shorter than the day before their birthday, for instance.

HOW TO HELP THEM LEARN TO MEASURE

Growing out of their clothes is a good occurrence to use to help children build awareness of size and measuring. They can compare clothes they've grown out of with ones that fit them now. They can compare both with their bigger siblings' clothes or with the baby's clothes.

Children can draw round everyone's hands and decide who has the biggest, whose hands are bigger than theirs, whose hands are smaller? Can they make someone's hands bigger or smaller? Can they also make someone's gloves bigger or smaller?

If they build something with construction blocks can they make *that* bigger? Can they make it longer or wider, etc?

How far can they hop or jump in one go? Can someone else hop or jump further? Or not so far?

What happens if they have a piece of Plasticene rolled into a ball and another one, identical, stretched into a long sausage? Which do they think is the biggest? Why? What about how heavy they are? Are they the same? Or different? Why?

Cooking, of course, is the ideal way for learning about weight and measurements. You can make cakes by using *cupfuls* – try making two or three mixtures with varying amounts of sugar and see what happens to the size and shape of the cakes when they're cooked. You'll see a drastic difference in the results. You can mix orange squash with different amounts of water and see what ha ppens. You can make sandwiches or pizzas using grated cheese – if they grate a piece of cheese do they think there is the same amount as before it was grated, or more, or less?

THE PRACTICAL ASPECTS OF THEIR LEARNING ABOUT MEASUREMENT

These questions, and the children's awareness are, once

again, all to do with *conservation*. The children can learn only by doing, not by you telling them. It is no good, for example, *telling* them and expecting them to understand, that although it took forty minutes to get to school yesterday when the traffic was bad, and it only took ten minutes today, it doesn't mean the distance was further yesterday. They have to assimilate, through experience and by developing their thinking skills, that the distance was still the same and that a *long time* doesn't necessarily mean a *long distance*.

TIME

The concept of time is really difficult for children to grasp. Part of the obstacle to their understanding is the fact that they haven't had much chance to experience time because their lives are so comparatively short. They just have not experienced much *time passing*.

Anyone of an older generation will tell you, 'The older you get, the quicker time passes'. Of course, time doesn't really pass more quickly, it's just there's much more of it behind us to cram into the memory bank.

HELP YOUR CHILDREN LEARN ABOUT TIME

Think about how quickly time seems to pass when you're having a good time, and how slowly it grinds along when you're bored and fed up. This happens to small children too, so the hour they spend with a friend may seem like a completely different span of time from the hour spent waiting for that friend to arrive.

Five minutes can pass in the twinkling of an eye when they're relishing that extra five minutes you promised them before bedtime, but it can seem like eternity when you've asked them to stay still for 'just five minutes' while you're browsing in the shops! It takes a lot of experience for children to realise that the measurement of 'five minutes' is the same each time.

HELP YOUR CHILD WITH THE LANGUAGE FOR TIME

There is a lot of language to learn for developing a concept of time. Some of the words or phrases your children need to learn are: today, tomorrow, yesterday, night, day, in a minute, morning, afternoon, last night, soon, later, later on, next week, before, after and when.

Even very young children quickly come to have some understanding of phrases like 'You can have a biscuit *after* lunch', 'You go to nursery *this afternoon*', 'We will go to the park *later on*'.

HELP YOUR CHILD TO UNDERSTAND THE CYCLICAL NATURE OF TIME

It takes a long time for a child to grasp the fact that things happen in order over long periods of time. For instance, if you've only ever had two birthdays, how can you begin to know what *a year* is?

Try to help your child by talking through regular events in your everyday life, such as getting up, going shopping, mealtimes, visiting Grandma, going to bed. Talk about things you did together *yesterday* and things you will do *tomorrow*. Stress the cyclical nature of things, and how routines happen in a particular order: 'We always have a story before we go to bed,' 'We always wash our hands before we have a meal,' 'We always put the toys away after we have played with them.'

HELPING YOUR CHILD GET READY TO 'TELL THE TIME'

Please don't try to teach your children how to 'tell the time' before they're ready. They need to know a lot before they can read a clock: the numbers 1 to 12; which hand is the minute hand, which is the hour; how to count in fives, both backwards and forwards; how an hour divides into twelve equal pieces. The more you try to hurry this skill, the more confused the children will become!

This doesn't mean that you can't help their development towards that skill, however. Concentrate on getting them familiar with time and the language that we use for time. You can do this by pointing out clocks and watches when you're out walking, telling them the time: 'Nearly nine o'clock – time for playschool!'; telling them how long they have to wait until their favourite programme comes on; checking the date on the calendar and talking about birthdays and special dates.

They can help with using egg-timers or setting a timer when you're cooking; they can observe the second hand go round on your watch a certain number of times, or time themselves against the minute hand on the clock to clear their toys away.

They can also mark off days on the calendar, and look forward to a day that has a special event. Count the days between, together, every day. Look at the calendar pictures of the seasons and the months and remind them about when it was snowing and when the sun was shining. All of these activities will help to build up a concept of time and its measurement that will hold them in good stead when they get to school.

HELP YOUR CHILD APPLY MATHS SKILLS

Implementing maths skills is all about applying logic and problem-solving to the job in hand. So, children who are sorting buttons may find all different ways of classifying them into groups of, say, colour, shape and size. They might then want to sort them into groups with two criteria, such as, all the big red ones and all the big green ones, all the flat green ones and all the flat yellow ones, and so on – button boxes can do wonders for children's maths!

Logical thinking allows the children to understand that, in order to build a high tower of bricks, they first need to build a foundation that will hold the tower.

Problem-solving may involve the children in working out how to sit the teddies in order of size or age or colour along the sofa, or how to make a café out of cardboard boxes. It's about trying and perhaps getting things wrong because the *thinking behind the task is not yet advanced enough* – the way to get things right is to learn by getting them wrong first. Children learn *because* of their mistakes, not in spite of them. Encourage them to try again, and again, because their knowledge and their thinking processes will develop with each endeavour.

Much of logical thinking and problem-solving is to do with patterns. Children eventually come to see the patterns in number, in sequence, in turns of events. To open their minds and their eyes to patterns you can help them to thread beads in colour or size patterns – 'Which one comes next?' – or build patterns with the construction blocks or make trails with different types of cars, or coloured cotton reels and arrange them in a pattern sequence, always helping the children to observe and understand the pattern and then continue it.

HELP YOUR CHILD EXPERIMENT AND OBSERVE

Young children learn mathematics in a very basic fashion, by doing and experimenting and observing – they are said to be in the stage of 'concrete operations'. This means that they need to be exploring and playing with tangible things – they are not yet able to take abstract propositions and unravel them. The more concrete exploration children have at this stage of their development, the better will be their maths skills when they eventually reach school – and it will show.

PRACTICAL ACTIVITIES

- Play lots of counting games, touching each thing as you count it.
- Count the plastic boats in the bath, take one away and count the ones that are left; count the blue flowers in the garden; count the cakes in the bun tray; count the cakes that are left when everyone has eaten one.
- Practise number rhymes together: One potato, two potato, three potato, four; Five little ducks went swimming one day; I saw three ships go sailing by; One, two, three, four, five, once I caught a fish alive; There were ten in the bed.
- Look for numbers on front doors, clocks, phones, clothing, buses, lift buttons, cars, calendars.
- Write numbers on gummed stickers, stick one to each of a set of toys (cars/dolls/boats etc) and line

them up in the right order.
- Count in tens, using beads on a thread, one penny pieces, bundles of crayons or buttons.
- Teach the names of the shapes in a shape posting-toy and the shapes of building blocks.
- Teach simple shape names – circle, round, square, oblong, triangle, cube, cylinder.
- Make biscuits, weighing out the ingredients carefully together.
- Fill yoghurt pots with sand/lentils/rice and watch what happens when you turn them out. What happens if they're wet?
- Use play scales to balance shells/leaves/rice/toy bricks etc.
- Use the bathroom scales to weigh each other and the dolls or teddies: Who's the heaviest? Who's the lightest? Do any weigh the same? What happens if the children weigh themselves, holding a teddy/ten teddies?
- Make jellies and turn the jellies out of the moulds; observe the jelly and the space it came from. Do the same with ice cubes and ice lollies.
- Make pastry and biscuits and cut out shapes. Look at the holes that are left behind. Will the shapes fit back in?
- Make monsters/cars/buildings out of construction kits; talk about the shapes, sizes and colours.
- Cut up gummed coloured paper and make patterns and mosaics.

Chapter Five

DEVELOPING CHILDREN'S INTELLECTUAL ABILITY

There has long been an argument about whether children are born with a certain amount of intellectual ability or 'intelligence', or whether it is a result of the way they are brought up. It's called the 'nature versus nurture' debate, and there probably will never be an end to it. In other words, it's beyond the realms of psychologists to know for certain the truth of the matter.

WHAT IS INTELLIGENCE?

Basically, whatever else it is, intelligence seems to be the ability to work things out, to solve problems, to learn – in other words, to think. The word 'intelligence' is a bit *passé* these days. Psychologists and educators prefer to speak in terms of 'learning ability', 'learning skills' and 'thinking skills'.

The key learning skills that contribute to 'intelligence' are the ability to process visual patterns, to recall previously heard information and to make comparisons. Intelligence tests, where they exist, are based on these skills and the resultant scores are compared with the typical scores of children of the same age.

THEORIES OF INTELLIGENCE

There are four basic theories of how children come to have intelligence. These are:

- that it is inherited – children are born with a fixed amount of intelligence, passed from their parents;
- that it is acquired – children depend on experience and stimulation during their formative years to develop intelligence;
- that it is interactive – children develop their intelligence as a result of the interaction between what they are born with and the experience and stimulation they receive in the early years;
- that it is learned – children can be taught how to think and, thus, how to become intelligent.

NO RIGHT ANSWER

Who is ever going to decide which of these theories is 'right'? Perhaps none of them is, but all of them are. Perhaps there's a little bit of truth in all of them and not the whole truth in any of them. Meanwhile, your child is growing and developing and you don't want her/him to be wasting any time in developing thinking and learning skills. What can you determine from the implications of any of the theories outlined above?

HOW DO CHILDREN DEVELOP INTELLECTUALLY?

Whichever theory or theories you feel you can go along with most happily, the implications for all of them are that all children:

• benefit from stimulation – they need intellectual challenges to move them on;
• need support – they want to feel valued and have someone interested in them in order to learn;
• tend to rise to positive, realistic expectations and, conversely, sink to the level of negative expectations;
• need to enjoy what they're doing: in order for them to learn you need to remove any tense atmosphere from the scene, otherwise they focus only on their feelings.

The fact is that, whichever theory you subscribe to, you *can* and *do* make a difference.

Action and Talk – The Most Effective Learning Method

The most effective way for children to learn is through action and talk. They gain information and make a breakthrough to conceptual knowledge by encountering the world they are trying to understand, in an active way. In other words, *doing* is essential to their learning. They explore, play and communicate their findings in talking about them. Every time they meet something new, they add it to the knowledge they already have.

At this stage – probably between birth and five years – children aren't able to understand abstract concepts. So, if you try to teach them that a sheep is a medium-sized animal with wool that grazes in a field, it won't mean much to them if they have never seen a field, let alone a sheep. But it might make a difference to their understanding if you take them to a children's farm and let them see, touch and smell the sheep in the field. They learn through what is called *concrete experience*.

CONCRETE EXPERIENCE

In terms of learning, 'concrete' almost means 'tangible' or 'active'. When children are counting, sorting and matching buttons, they are learning abstract concepts with the help of concrete, or tangible materials – the buttons. When they are playing in the bath, they are learning about the properties of water – that things can float or sink in it, that it finds its own level, that it can be poured. They are again learning abstract concepts with concrete, or tangible materials – the water, funnels, jugs, containers – and by active participation – doing things.

ACTIVE LEARNING

You don't have to provide dozens and dozens of expensive, highly-coloured, 'educationally sound' toys for your children to become active learners. In fact, in many ways quite the opposite is true.

The problem with a great many 'designed' toys is that they have a function and an objective and they can not really be used for anything else. Thus, once a child has explored the usefulness of an action toy, its usefulness may be over. Whereas once the child has explored the usefulness of, say, the cardboard box that the new washing-machine came packed in, there might be so much more to find out that you're impelled to get hold of another cardboard box on the demise of the first one!

Everyone knows the joke about Grandma buying the most expensive toy ever for the child's birthday, and the child playing with the wrapping. It's not a fallacy; it's fact, because often the child can do so much more with the wrapping in terms of exploration and discovery, than will ever be possible with the expensive toy.

LEARNING ON HIS/HER OWN

Children learn very well by their own efforts. They don't need you on hand all the time. Given problems to solve, they will attempt to solve them by exploration and discovery. Once they've achieved their solution, they'll often move onwards in an attempt to discover more. Picture the child playing in the bath who wants to fill the shampoo bottle with water. The child may try over and over again to fill it by using a spoon or a small object, only to find that the water escapes before it gets into the shampoo bottle. Much exploration may result in the use of a jug with a lip, or a funnel. More exploration will show the child that if the bottle's held firmly under the water it can fill itself. All of this knowledge adds on to what the child already knows and builds up concepts of water and receptacles.

Of course, if you are there you can help the child to develop the language that goes with the concept by talking through the activity, adding more and more vocabulary – *drop, splash, spill, wet, pour, sink, float* etc.

THE IMPORTANCE OF LANGUAGE

Thinking comes before speaking – children always understand a lot more in these early stages than they can put into words. You can test this out by giving them instructions. Children just learning to toddle will enjoy carrying out instructions like 'Go and tickle Mummy's knee,' 'Put the feather on your head,' 'Give Daddy a kiss,' well before they can actually verbalise those instructions back to you.

But the more language you put in, the more comes out. In fact, to develop their thinking skills what you really need to give them is language, language and more language. Why?

EVEN LIMITED USE IS HELPFUL

Developing children are still trying to make sense of the world. One of the ways in which they try to do this is to make some kind of intelligible framework for it. So they put what they do into words: 'I put the water in the jug and it all spilled out when I tried to get it in the top of the bottle, because the bottle wasn't big enough. But when I got the funnel and put the little end in the bottle, the water went in OK.' If they haven't got the language to make this framework they make as near an approximation to it as they can. But if they *have* got the language it's easier for them to form a concept.

Remember that the concept may not be fully formed. It is a part-awareness, if you like. But the next time they meet the same ideas, that part-awareness becomes knowledge which they already have and, from what they learn on the present meeting, they add more knowledge. Their learning is a continuous process.

THE PARENTAL ROLE

These early years are of crucial importance to your growing child's life. During the first five years, children learn more and at a faster rate than they will ever learn again. It's an exciting and challenging time – it is the time that establishes the foundations of all future development. Your help and encouragement can make all the difference in the world to that development.

HOW YOU CAN USE OBSERVATION TO HELP THEM

Of course, no one suggests that you spend all your time trying to 'feed in knowledge' to the children! But just by being aware of how they learn you will begin to see the patterns of behaviour they go through – possibly over and over again – in order to form a concept. Nothing is learned in one fell swoop Often the children are in the process of forming many different concepts simultaneously. So while they are learning about the properties of water, they may also be learning about shapes and sizes – *some jugs are thin and long, some are wide and squat, big jugs hold more water than little ones*, etc.

Take a couple of steps back and observe your children at play. Try to work out for yourself what problems they are trying to solve, what they are actually finding out about or learning at the given moment. Once you understand that, you can help by gentle questioning and by offering more vocabulary.

HELPING YOUR CHILD TO CONCENTRATE

There's a case for helping children to develop the powers of concentration and attentiveness that they'll need once they get to nursery or to school.

Concentration is something that develops from birth onwards. Often you will find that, as toddlers, the children seem to go from one toy to another, one activity to another, without ever really finishing one thing before they're started on the next.

Sometimes children are so inquisitive, so bent on making this construction of the world around them, that they just flit from one thing to another without ever stopping to wait and think. On the one hand it's good to have children who are highly motivated and curious, of course, but on the other they will need to be able to pay attention and get absorbed in things if they are not to flounder when they begin nursery or school.

You can help them to develop their concentration skills by regularly and gently encouraging them to stay and finish one thing before they go off to something else. Somehow you need to instil the idea that they don't start off on something else before finishing the first thing; that the next thing will wait until they are ready. You can help by insisting that they sit still and stay to finish meals; or courses of meals, that they stay and listen to the end of the story; that they finish painting one picture before starting another.

Concentration will improve gradually, but you certainly can't do any harm by helping it along in a gentle but firm way. Again, don't expect it to happen overnight. But even if you don't think you're getting anywhere, just keep going and allow time for change to happen.

HELP THEM BUILD A BANK OF KNOWLEDGE

The best way to build up your children's bank of knowledge, and thus their thinking skills, is to involve them in activities as much as possible, and talk through those activities as they're happening, or afterwards.

You don't have to spend lots of money taking them to special places – theme parks, shows, Disneyland. Family events and shared walks and enterprises are just as good – in fact they may be better.

TEACHING THROUGH FAMILY EVENTS

For children, one of the most interesting points of learning about families is how everyone has so many different roles. Their mother may also be somebody's sister, somebody's daughter, somebody's niece. This kind of information absolutely fascinates them, and it helps to build up the many patterns that give them insight into the world.

Even very small children can understand some of these different roles – they are often amazed that their parents are their grandparents' children: how can they be, when they are not children at all? Try to make games out of giving this kind of family information. Ask them, 'Who's Sarah's daddy to me, then?' 'Who am I to Grandad?' etc.

Through family events they will also begin to learn the way the years come round. Families often gather for birthdays and other festivities. You can talk about 'Do you remember when . . . ?' and 'Next week, when it's Daddy's birthday . . .'. Thus, they're learning about time and the way things come around and around.

You can also make books with family photographs, getting the children to help you write the captions for them. This will help them to put into words the way the people are related to each other and also the events which you have shared. Print the captions clearly for them in black felt pen, underneath the photos, and use the book as a special 'reading' book that you can share. While you're looking at it and talking about it together, you can feed in lots of language and help them to verbalise their experiences.

TEACHING THROUGH WALKS IN YOUR OWN ENVIRONMENT

Going for walks is not a passive thing to do. To begin with, discuss where you are going and what route you may take. You can let the children choose: 'Which way shall we go?' Why do they want to go that way? What might you pass? What might you see? Who might you bump into on the way?

Talk about the environment as you walk through it. Do you live in a town? a city? a suburb? the country-side? the seaside? by a river? in a built-up area? Try to explain something of the background to your environment to the children. Say to them, 'Remember when we stayed at the seaside? It was different from this, wasn't it? Can you remember how it was different?' or 'When we go on our holidays, we'll stay on a farm. It won't be like this. There will be . . .' etc.

Point out things that are happening that make changes in the environment. For example, the weather will probably be different from the last time you walked the same route. Maybe the season has changed. Talk about what's different about the season. Say, for example, 'Remember in summer when there were lots of leaves on the trees? Now they're all turning brown and are falling off. That's because it's autumn now.'

Talk about trees being trees, hedges being hedges and flowers being flowers. Point out the differences between different kinds of vegetation. Look for special things – green leaves, yellow flowers, flat pebbles.

It doesn't matter whether you think this kind of information is going way over their heads, the important thing is to enjoy the walk and to answer any questions that your information prompts. Also, remember they are using their senses to explore the environment that you're describing, so they are building up some kind of awareness that will be added to later, when they have more conceptual knowledge.

Look out for animals – even if they're only domestic ones – and talk about them: 'How many legs have they got? Do they have tails? Have they got fur, feathers or shells? How do they move? Do they run and jump? Do they fly, or slither? Do you know what kind of noise they make? What do you think they eat?' When you get home, compare the animals you saw outside with animals in the children's books, or with those of the toy farm or other toys they might have. What can they find that's the same? What can they find that's different?

Look for shadows – young children are fascinated by them. Get them to experiment with their own shadow and yours. Ask them, 'Is your shadow bigger than you or smaller? Can you fix your shadow on to somebody else's shadow? Can you make a jumping shadow? Can you get away from your shadow? What do you think makes your shadow?' If they can't guess what causes shadows, tell them. Show them how the shadow changes shape and size as the sun goes round. Next time they meet shadows they'll remember some of this discovery and will add further to their knowledge.

Look out for things that move on wheels. How many different kinds of wheeled transport can they think of before you start your walk? Can they draw them and tick them off as they see them, or make a tally of how many of each vehicle they see? Have they got toys at home which they can compare?

Talk about the different kinds of buildings you see on your walk: what are they for? Who might be in them? Can they build some of these buildings with their blocks or construction toys when you get home?

TEACHING THROUGH THE GARDEN

You don't need to have a beautiful, huge garden with sweeping lawns to teach your children about the outdoors. The smallest plot or bit of yard will do.

For a start, watch the different kinds of weather – how do they affect your garden? Put out buckets to catch the rain or snow and see how much you've caught each day. What happens when it gets really cold? What happens to the snow when it gets warmer? Can they pick icicles from the window ledges in the winter?

There are lots of things that are really easy to grow, and all you need is a bit of space, a seed tray perhaps, a bucket or plant pot and a bit of compost. Try beans, lettuce, radishes or grass. Try taking cuttings from shrubs, dip them in hormone rooting powder, put them in a pot, water it and cover it with a plastic bag secured with a rubber band. Watch the shrub begin to grow, then plant it out or re-pot it into a larger pot.

Try planting different vegetable and fruit seeds – apple, orange, a conker, an acorn, a peanut or marrow seeds. Plant a potato in a bucket filled with compost and watch what happens over a period of time. This 'waiting to see' is important in itself, as children have to learn that results or gratification can't always be instant.

Encourage the children to make their own garden in a wooden box balanced on bricks, or in a large pot. They can have a lot of success with bulbs or bedding plants, and they'll feel really proud when their flowers grow and thrive. Encourage them to water the flowers when necessary, and keep them going all through the growing period so their gardens don't come to harm.

Make or buy a bird table and encourage wild birds to your patch for the children to observe. You can make good winter bird food by chopping up bacon rinds, crumbling bread, and mixing the whole lot together in a bowl with suet, banana, sultanas, raisins, peanut butter, margarine, a few chopped nuts and sunflower seeds. Stir it all together and put it out on your bird-table, or on the ground if you haven't got one. For the birds who like to swing as they're eating, put some of the mixture in a lemon or onion netting bag and hang it from a tree, the fence or the bird-table. Then stand back and watch the action.

TEACHING IN THE HOUSE

Your imagination is the only limit to the kinds of thing that you can teach your child in the house. In the kitchen, they can indulge in water play and 'cook' with you. They don't have to be involved with the whole of the menu – for example, just whisking the eggs or making egg white turn into a frothy mountain may be enough to consider for one session.

Don't stop at just 'looking'. Make use of all of their senses as much as you can. They can taste, smell, listen and touch as well as look. The more you teach them to use all their senses, the more you'll contribute to their intellectual development. Shake the peppercorns, rice, lentils and the tin of custard to listen to the different sounds they make. Smell the cakes before they're baked, while they're baking and after they've baked. Get your children to identify what you might be cooking from its aroma. Get them to identify what utensils you're using by their sounds.

Children can help organise cupboards, working out what fits where and how much more can go in. Perhaps you move the furniture around from time to time – talk about the possibilities with them: what will the room look like if the furniture is moved? Draw a picture of it, decide whether it would be a good idea or not, and think about why.

Set up a little shop, using boxes and packages etc from the store cupboard. You can make your own play-dough quite easily to mould vegetables and fruit. You need 3 cups of flour, 3 cups of water, 2 tablespoons of cream of tartar, 2 cups of salt and 2 tablespoons of oil. Mix all the dry ingredients, then add the water and the oil. Cook it in a pan, over a medium heat, stirring it all the time until it becomes very firm and hot. Roll it out on a floured surface, fold it and knead it until it has a flexible consistency. Store it in an airtight container.

You can make your own finger paints by mixing 3 tablespoons of sugar, half a cup of cornflower and 2 cups of cold water. Stir the mixture over a low heat until it begins to thicken and turn glossy. Add a tablespoon of washing-up liquid. Put the mixture into yoghurt pots and add a variety of food colourings to them.

Use the kitchen scales to weigh and measure dry materials (rice/lentils etc) and explore pouring them. The children will play for hours just experimenting, and will be happy to come back to the same kind of play days or weeks later (when they will 'add on' to what they have already found out). It might mean a bit of mess, but the vacuum cleaner will sort that out, and the children will have learned lots from their research.

You can make all kinds of buildings or vehicles out of cardboard boxes taken from the supermarket or appliance stores. All you need is a pair of scissors or a sharp knife, some paint, Sellotape and a bit of imagination. Once you begin to show the children what a box can become, their imagination will take over. Use really large boxes to make a playhouse or a garage, a fire station, an aeroplane hangar, a spaceship etc, where they can role-play to their heart's content. Turn slightly smaller boxes upside-down and paint on wheels to make buses, taxis or trains. Use small boxes, painted and with and a few circular bits or little boxes stuck on, to make little cookers, or make kitchen cupboards, beds for nursing teddies or whatever.

To make a playhouse, turn a large box upside-down. Before you cut, ask the children where they want the doors and windows and get them to decide what size and shape they'll be. Get them to help draw them in with a black felt pen and a ruler (but banish them from the area when you do the cutting). Once the cutting is completed, you can all pitch in to paint the house: give the children as much choice as you can (try to find old paints from the garage) and let them get on with it.

Tents are always good fun. You don't have to spend much money – a sheet over the table is as good as anything and it's quickly cleared up when necessary. The whole point of tents is the hiding away, building a little world that nobody else is in (unless it's a friend), so give them the materials and let them get on with it.

Pegs and buttons provide lots of opportunity for developing key maths skills – even the simple act of putting pegs from one box into another, or into a bag, or into several boxes, can keep children absorbed and learning for ages. Remember that when they're showing this length of absorption it's because their minds are reflecting and working it all out, and that means they are learning and developing their intellectual ability.

Button boxes may have gone out of fashion but, as already mentioned, they are invaluable tools for sorting and matching. You can easily gather lots of buttons together by chopping them off thrown-out clothing or buying them cheaply: they will still cost very little in comparison with brightly-coloured plastic materials that serve the same educational purpose, bought from a commercial retailer, and the children will be fascinated by them. Apart from sorting and matching they can make up little stories – Who had this button on what? Where were they going . . . ? etc.

Routines and rituals that you follow in the home are excellent for promoting the idea of sequence in children's minds. They begin to learn that when you do that, this happens; when you have had this event, that event occurs. They learn about the way things go round in time and about cause and effect and this knowledge again contributes to their intellectual development.

Even chores like defrosting the freezer are brilliant learning experiences for little children – Where did all the ice come from? What's going to happen to it now?

YOU DON'T HAVE TO SPEND YOUR LIFE *TEACHING*
Of course, none of this means that you have to spend

ninety-nine per cent of your life teaching your children. You don't have to be consumed with trying to help them progress and feeling guilty if you're not 'doing something with them'. Most of the time you can help them set something up and then leave them to get on with it, especially if they have friends or siblings with them.

As you get into the way of thinking that allows you to see what your children are learning from the activities you set up or share, you will begin to see opportunities – for input, for intervention, for language – and you will quite naturally make the most of those opportunities. The teaching will become almost second nature to you, so it shouldn't be confused with 'putting on the pressure' or trying to get your children to 'perform'.

CHILDREN AND GUILT

Don't feel guilty if you have to go to work and leave your children to carers while you're not about. Just try to choose a childcarer who knows as much about child development as you. Try to pick one, for example, who has plenty of activities planned for the child and knows a bit about how important language development and routine are for children, and who doesn't expect them to sit still and watch television all day. Then, just try to make the most of the time you have with them yourself.

In the last analysis you have to accept that your children are who *they* are and you are who *you* are: in the long run you're merely giving them a helping hand.

PRACTICAL ACTIVITIES

- Try to provide a stimulating environment, with lots

of things to do and think about, but not so much at once that it's overwhelming.
- Vary the activities you do together as much as you can within the children's routine, and encourage their involvement in basic chores.
- Take some toys/games away at different times, and bring them back later when they've been 'forgotten'.
- Play a wide range of board and activity games that need turn-taking and sharing.
- If they face a problem that's too hard to solve, try breaking it down into smaller components.
- Teach your children their name, age and address as soon as they can learn and remember it.
- Encourage them to want to make things out of play-dough, Plasticene, papier mâché or cardboard boxes.
- Look at things in the natural world together – grass, shells, leaves, flowers, rocks, twigs, insects and animals. Get children's books from the library to help back up their observations.
- Make collections of things they like – shells, bits of material, feathers, leaves, fir cones etc. Let them keep their 'precious things' in a special box or special place.
- Teach them about looking after the environment, such as not throwing litter on the floor, and caring for pets and other animals.
- When you're out walking, use spatial concepts in your language, such as 'over the road', 'across the bridge', 'under the tunnel'.
- You can make almost anything into a meaningful learning experience – at this age, children are learning something every moment of the day. It's up to you to exploit the possibilities of what they're experiencing.

Chapter Six

PHYSICAL DEVELOPMENT

You only have to think of how much varied movement children learn to make between birth and five years to realise that they need a lot of exercise. Movement is learned with practice, and all physical activity promotes the healthy growth of bones, muscles, the heart and lungs. The movements children make are controlled through *motor skills* and these are divided basically into two categories – *gross motor skills* and *fine motor skills*.

GROSS MOTOR SKILLS

Gross motor skills are those which children use to walk, run, climb, jump, clamber, crawl, hop, skip and dance – all of the movements which use large muscles.

FINE MOTOR SKILLS

Fine motor skills are used for controlled manipulation of hands, fingers, toes or small muscles – all the skills children need to be able to dress themselves, write, paint, draw or wiggle their fingers and toes.

WHICH COMES FIRST?
Gross motor control always precedes fine motor

control. This means that children need to get control over their large body movements before they can begin to master the manipulation of small objects like pencils, child scissors, bead-threaders etc.

RATE OF DEVELOPMENT

You should always bear in mind that all children develop at different rates and two children can be at completely different stages of physical development even though they are the same chronological age. This is quite normal. Children grow and progress quite instinctively during their formative years, and mostly they will develop without any need to worry at all.

However, if you always provide encouragement and help, you can help them use the skills they already have, to practise them and move on to the next stage. Avoid putting on too much pressure as this can overwhelm children. Physical development is like development in all the other areas – if you break the tasks down into small activities they are more likely to achieve success.

SHOWING THEM WHAT TO DO

In terms of physical control and developing motor skills, the 'sitting next to Nellie' way of teaching has everything going for it. When children are especially independent and resistant to offers of help, they will be much more willing to have a go at something if they can see you doing it – whether it's throwing or kicking a ball or trying to hop all the way down the garden. By demonstrating the activity in a playing kind of way, you will make the children want to attempt it too.

HOW CHILDREN DEVELOP
GROSS MOTOR SKILLS

During their first year, babies are motivated to investigate their immediate surroundings by their curiosity and their attempts to understand the world. Encourage them to: reach out, roll over, crawl, shuffle, sit and, if they show readiness, stand and maybe walk.

In their second year they become bigger, stronger, more independent and inquisitive. Encourage them to: crawl rapidly, pull themselves up, fall backwards to sit, walk by themselves, balance and bend to pick things up, climb stairs and furniture, try to jump from two feet to two feet, walk confidently, and dance to music.

In their third year they have increasing confidence and explore all kinds of ways of moving. Encourage them to: clamber up, over, through and around large objects; gain control of whole-body actions such as running, jumping, balancing, throwing and kicking; run and stop with some control; stretch and curl up to alter their body shape and balance and move on tiptoe.

By the time they are four, most children are increasingly confident and adventurous in what they do. They have good co-ordination and control and learn to do more things with their bodies practically every day. By now they should be able to try: running and stopping with good control; jumping, getting higher and higher elevation; balancing on one foot; hopping from one foot to the other and, for a short period of time, hopping on one foot without losing their balance; tiptoeing, marching, striding, creeping, crawling and galloping; shrinking and stretching into different shapes; curling up small and rolling sideways; walking backwards and moving in circles and lines.

All of these movements will be learned in response to their environment. Thus, if you give them a huge cardboard box or a toy to practise clambering in and out of, they will develop those skills; if you encourage them to walk instead of sitting in the push-chair or being carried, they will develop their co-ordination and muscular skills; if you visit safe, open spaces such as a park, where they can run freely, they will learn control.

On the other hand, of course, if you try at all times to 'keep them safe' or 'under control' and are afraid to let them experiment or do things for themselves, their motor skills will take much longer to develop.

HOW CHILDREN DEVELOP FINE MOTOR SKILLS

From about three months and during their first year, babies begin to show interest in things around them. Encourage them to: reach out for toys in front of them or just out of their reach; close their fingers around a small object; hold a rattle and shake it a few times; wiggle their hands and fingers as they watch them; hold a small toy in each hand; loose a toy from their grasp; control hand movements with more co-ordination – for example, they will understand that if they have a toy in each hand and you pass them another one, they will have to drop one to grasp it; play purposefully with two toys together, for example, banging one on the other, or placing one on top of the other; crumple up paper and lift a cup or other object from their food tray.

During their second year, encourage them to: hold a brick in each hand and bang the two together; do pat-a-cake; wave goodbye; pick things up using their thumb and forefinger in a pincer grip; drop things from a pincer grip; begin to feed themselves; grip two things in each hand; open boxes; complete an inset board puzzle; hold a drink; build five or more bricks and pick up very small objects, for instance, peas.

During their third year, encourage them to: turn the pages of books; thread laces on a card; thread beads; scribble with different tools (crayons/chalks/paints); draw lines and circles; help to dress and undress themselves; manipulate child scissors; do small jigsaws; draw simple pictures and stick gummed paper into spaces.

WHAT CHILDREN NEED TO BUILD UP THESE SKILLS

During all this time of building up their gross and fine motor skills children are literally and metaphorically learning to stand on their own two feet. To do this they need to build up body awareness – that is, to become alert to all the different things the different parts of their bodies can do and allow them to do; to build confidence – that is, the ability to explore and experiment without being frightened; and to build up control – that is, the ability to regulate their movements in ways appropriate to whatever situation they are in.

YOUR ROLE IN HELPING THE DEVELOPMENT OF MOTOR SKILLS

START AS SOON AS YOU CAN

It's never too soon to begin introducing children to

physical games that will help them to develop their motor skills. For example, babies respond quickly and inquisitively to mirrors placed where they can see themselves, and will be curious about the movement they can see. They love dangling, brightly-coloured or sparkling mobiles that they can reach out or up to, and branches or clouds that move above their prams. Their curiosity is also fed by watching other people move about so, for example, give them lots of opportunity to watch you working in the kitchen or the garden.

Use their wakeful moments to play finger and toe action games (*see Practical Activities*). They love gentle rocking rhymes, such as 'Hush-a-bye baby', 'See-saw, Margery Daw' and 'Baa-baa, black sheep'. They also enjoy bouncing rhymes such as 'Yankee Doodle' and 'Ride-a-cock-horse', where you sit them on your knee, facing you, holding them at the waist with two hands, then bounce gently up and down together to the rhythm of the words and music.

When your baby can sit up, sit on the floor with your own legs wide open. Sit the baby in front of you so that he/she is just propped against you in case you're needed as a cushion to stop them falling backwards. Put toys on the floor in front of them and encourage them to lean forwards to pick them up. This will help them to develop balancing skills.

HELPING THEM ON TO THEIR FEET

You can help babies get on their feet by giving them lots of 'feet awareness' exercise, that is, when they start feeling their feet, encourage them and help them to understand that their feet are part of them.

A good exercise is for you to sit with your legs wide apart with the baby sitting on one of your thighs, baby's feet firmly on the ground in between your legs. This sitting position gives them a starting point for standing. Encourage them to try to stand and then sit back down on your leg. Have your arms ready for support, so that you may have one arm in front of them for holding on to and one hand gently at their back. When they get quite good at this, push your legs together and let the legs help to balance them rather than your hands.

Baby bouncers and walkers are a matter of personal choice. Remember, though, that babies need to learn to balance themselves rather than having something else do the job for them and they cannot begin to walk until they have achieved a really good feel for balancing.

Walking round the furniture is the normal route to taking first steps. If your baby seems happy to pull him/herself up and stand at the furniture, but doesn't seem to want to move, you can show him/her how to do it by gently moving one foot to the side, then the other foot along to it. Continue for several steps. You may need to help with the arm movements as well. Walking sideways first is the normal pattern so help the baby to get the idea of this before attempting to walk forwards, simply because it is not a good idea to miss out any of the process.

IMPROVING BALANCE AND CO-ORDINATION

There are lots of things you can do to help your children develop balance and co-ordination. One of the best things is to encourage them to play with other children. They will very quickly begin to display lots of resourceful behaviour that will involve good physical movement. They will play imaginative games together in which they rely on movement as a means of communication and expression. They will run, dodge, dart from space to space and become increasingly confident and adventurous in the things they do.

Playing with other children is very important because it gives them an incentive to join in and motivates them to do the same things that others are doing.

The more space they have to move around in, the better. They'll learn about their bodies in relation to space, other people and objects through having a large area to run, jump and climb in. This will help them to develop the concept of spatial awareness and gain confidence in moving in their environment. Try to find a safe park where they can explore the climbing frame and other outdoor equipment. Encourage them to ride tricycles and push-cars or pedal cars and to enjoy the walk to the park as much as the park activity itself.

Don't push your children to do more than they feel physically capable of doing at any time, just help them gently to explore the equipment or games in the way that they feel able. If, for example, they are too scared to climb up the steps of a slide, encourage them to climb up two or three then take them off, saying 'Well done!' and try for another step the next day. Lots of practice and plenty of time to feel confident in their balance will give them the poise they need to progress. Remember, there's no hurry, life and learning isn't a race.

MAKE YOUR OWN EQUIPMENT
With a little bit of imagination you can easily make

play equipment at home to encourage co-ordination and balance. For example:

• use a washing-line or rope as a 'snake' and ask the children to walk along it; walk with one foot each side of it; walk across it in a zigzag and jump across it;
• balance a piece of wood on two stacks of books or house bricks, just one brick high, and encourage them to walk along it. Hold their hand if they are not   confident. Get them to walk it with one foot on and one foot off. Get them to do 'fairy steps' (toe to heel, toe to heel) along it. When they're really good, get them to walk backwards along it;
• give them something to balance on their heads as they move – it might be a large plastic bowl, a small beanbag (or bean-filled toy) or a teddy. You can make this slightly harder by getting them to clap their hands while they're walking, or by getting them to march or walk backwards;
• do steps across the pavement, missing out the cracks. Alternatively, walk only on the cracks;
• walk along low walls, doing different walks, such as strides, tiptoe, 'fairy footsteps';
• lean one end of a plank of wood against a step and encourage or help your child to crawl and then walk up and down the sloping plank.

Of course, you must make sure that none of the things you have set up are likely to be dangerous, and stay with your child to supervise.

MAKE UP YOUR OWN GAMES
You can also make up games involving lots of physical

activity, which the children will enjoy playing just with you almost as much as with a group of other children:

- walk forwards, backwards and sideways, and with a small beanbag/cuddly toy on your heads. See whose beanbag falls off first;
- stand with a small beanbag on your head and try to sit down without it falling off. If you manage it, try to stand up again;
- play 'musical statues' together. Play some music to which you walk, hop, skip or dance. Freeze into statues when the music stops (which you'll have to make it do);
- try hop-racing along the room, first on one foot, then the other;
- do follow-my-leader silly walks, such as crouching down and swinging your arms; bending at the knees; doing four steps and a jump or marching like a soldier. Encourage the children to be leaders sometimes;
- see how many different parts of the body you can both balance on. Can you balance on one leg, one leg and two hands, your bottom and one foot, two hands and one foot, your side, your bottom alone? You may be able to think of lots more fun ways to balance – encourage your child to use her/his imagination.

These kinds of games are simple, but they never lose their attraction for the children because each time they join in, they find that they can push themselves just a little bit further, or achieve just a little bit more.

THROWING AND CATCHING GAMES
You can start throwing and catching games quite early,

but bear in mind that children need to have developed a lot of co-ordination, balance and manual dexterity to have much control.

In a way it's far better for adults to be involved in throwing and catching games, because children find it quite difficult to throw accurately to each other and this makes it even more difficult for the child catching.

Choose your materials carefully. Small beanbags are excellent for throwing and catching, and much easier for little hands to manipulate than balls. By the same token, small balls are much better for practising kicking than football-sized balls, which are too large and often too hard for small children to kick.

In the absence of anything else, screwed-up newspaper makes an ideal substitute for a ball, and a large cardboard box with no lid makes a perfect container for throwing the missiles into. A hoop leaned against a wall or laid on the ground is also good.

Try to encourage the children not to compete with each other, but with themselves, so that they're striving against their own previous performance – for example, two beanbags in the hoop one week, three the next.

The same with catching. Get the child to sit or stand, and encourage them to follow the object you are throwing with their eyes. Often they watch their hands, hoping that the beanbag will land in them. They have to learn the art of keeping their eyes on the ball, and it takes a long time for this co-ordination to develop. Don't be down-hearted if you think the children are making no headway. Remember, it is practice that will establish the skill eventually.

DEVELOPING FINE MOTOR CONTROL

Probably the first thing babies do towards developing fine motor skills is to track a moving object with their eyes. They will begin to do this very early on, when you hold a small toy in your hand and attract the baby's attention with it. Move the toy gently round and round and the baby will watch it. After a while you will find that it's possible to put a small rattle or toy in the baby's hand and shake it gently a few times. The baby will carry on holding it for a little while.

At about six months babies are able to hold a toy or other object in each hand. If you hold a rattle or sound toy just out of reach and make a noise with it they will respond to the sound. Ask them to take the toy from you. If it drops from their grasp, ask them where it has gone, and try to get them to follow it with their eyes.

Babies usually show a lot of interest in their fingers and toes. Encourage this play, touch their fingers and hands, toes and feet in different ways and try to build up their awareness of these parts of their body.

ACTIVITIES THAT CONTRIBUTE TO THE DEVELOPMENT OF FINE MOTOR SKILLS

Almost any activity that allows children to use their hands and fingers is making a contribution to their fine motor skill development.

Encourage them to help dress/undress themselves as soon as they show any inclination to co-operate with you. It's very easy to make the excuse to yourself that it takes too long, you're in a rush, they can't manipulate the bits and pieces – but in the long run you're only doing them a disservice by making these excuses.

The more they learn to control their dressing and undressing, the more their skills develop. Find things with different kinds of fastening – buttons and button-holes, velcro, zips, press studs, ties – that you can play games of dressing-up or dressing the toys with. Encourage these games, because the children will get plenty of practice at all the fiddly little things fingers have to do to achieve control of the fasteners, and this will stand them in good stead when they eventually have to go to school and look after themselves.

Likewise with their water play, sand play, pasta and rice play in the kitchen: though they may accidentally knock containers over regularly, or spill the contents, the more you encourage them to practise, the better. If they don't practise they're not suddenly going to wake up one morning able to tip a measure of lentils from one container to another with perfect hand–eye co-ordination and muscle control. To reach that objective they need to have been able, and allowed, to make all the mistakes and do all the knocking over, tipping and spilling necessary for developing a skill.

Toddlers really enjoy ripping up paper. They like the sound it makes and it's good for fine muscle control because of the actions they have to make with their fingers to grip and tear. Give them old magazines and brochures and, if you recycle your papers, remember they're still fit for recycling when they're in pieces!

As soon as the children can hold a crayon or paint-brush, get them interested in making marks on paper. At first they will hold the tool in a kind of fist, but show them how to hold it between their thumb and fingers. They'll need lots of practice at this before they're really

103

competent, but that's OK – it's practice that's important.

To begin with, children often seem to be quite ambidextrous, but eventually they will begin to show preference for one hand or the other. Don't worry if they appear to be left-handed, just help them to strengthen their preferred hand. It's not a good idea to try to force them to use their right hand. Most left-handed people have a dominant left eye, and compelling them to use their right hand leads to great confusion.

Give them lots of experience with plenty of different drawing and writing implements. Just let them be free to explore and practise. You can use the back of rolls of unused wallpaper to create lovely big pictures on, or just scribbles. Try using big fat wax crayons, thin wax crayons, felt pens, pencil crayons, pencils, chalk, thick paint-brushes, thin paint-brushes, even straws and bits of string dipped in paint.

The more variety the children get, the better will be their control and their flow when they come to doing what many educationists consider to be the real work of fine motor control – writing! And, whatever you do, try to keep it up. This does not mean day in, day out drill, it just means having fun and making physical activity a part of the children's play lives. The big thing to remember about skills is that they're gained with practice and they quickly deteriorate without any!

Remember, also, that one of the most important things is to keep *talking* and encouraging the children to talk through these activities. They need to learn the vocabulary for the activities and they need to be able to explain and to describe them – language is just as important to physical activities as to everything else!

PRACTICAL ACTIVITIES

FINGER AND TOE GAMES:
Here is the church
(Touch fists together at knuckles)
Here is the steeple
(Open fists and touch fingertips together)
Open the doors
(Open hands wide)
And here are the people
(Wriggle fingers)
Here is the parson going upstairs
(Walk fingers upwards into the air)
And here he is, a-saying his prayers
(Put hands together for prayer)

Round and round the garden, like a teddy bear
(Draw circles on the palm of baby's hand with your finger)
One step, two steps,
(Tiptoe with your fingers along baby's arm)
Tickly under there!
(Tickle baby in a ticklish spot)

Two little dickie-birds sitting on a wall
(Make beak shapes with first finger and thumb of each hand)
One named Peter, one named Paul
(Open and close each beak in turn)
Fly away, Peter! Fly away, Paul!
(Flutter each hand into the air and behind your back)
Come back, Peter! Come back, Paul!
(Flutter each hand back again)

This little piggy went to market   *(Hold baby's big toe)*
This little piggy stayed at home   *(Hold second toe)*
This little piggy had roast beef   *(Hold third toe)*
This little piggy had none   *(Hold fourth toe)*
And this little piggy went wee-wee-wee all the way
home!   *(Run your finger along baby's body to a ticklish spot and tickle)*

FOR GROSS MOTOR CONTROL

• Play 'Simon Says', giving the children different shapes to put their bodies into ('Make a star', 'Make a tall, thin shape') or different actions to do ('Stand on one foot', 'Put your arms out in front of you').
• Play 'What's this bit called?' to teach the names of all the body parts, as the child's dressing and undressing.
• Help them to get the idea of jumping by putting a piece of string on the floor and getting them to step over it with one foot, then two.
• Act out nursery rhymes together, such as 'Jack and Jill' going up the hill or 'Little Miss Muffet', etc.
• Play 'Here We Go Round the Mulberry Bush' and do all their normal daily routine actions ('This is the way we clean our teeth/brush our hair/put on our shoes').
• Play 'Ring-a-Roses'.
• When you're going for a walk, take opportunities to change your pace so that they experience moving very slowly, moving very quickly, darting etc.
• Do silly direction walks, so that instead of walking in a straight line you walk in a zigzag, or a circle, and they have to follow you. Do this also with movements other than walking, such as hopping or skipping.

FOR FINE MOTOR CONTROL

• Make pastry and biscuits. Let the children cut out the shapes and place them on the baking trays.

• Paint with finger paints – make portraits of the family and hang them in the kitchen.

• Draw pictures of favourite toys. Cut them out and stick them into a scrapbook.

• Make pompoms together. You need two rings of cardboard, placed together. Thread wool around the outside and through the middle, around and through, until there is a whole pad of wool around the rings. Cut the wool at the outside between the two pieces of card. Tie a piece of wool tightly between the rings to hold the wool together in the centre. Remove the rings and fluff up the pompom.

• Make pictures with pasta shapes, lentils and melon seeds etc, glued on to card.

• Cut out shapes from coloured sticky paper to make faces on paper plates.

• Cut out snowflakes from a circular piece of paper folded in half, then half again. Cut little holes in the paper on the folds, then unfold to see your snowflake.

• Thread things – beads, buttons, bits of pasta – on to different thicknesses of thread.

• Do printing with leaves, cotton reels, bits of Lego.

• Save small cardboard packets and encourage your child to open and close the little flaps, to unfold them and fold them back up again.

• Look out for toys with winding and screwing applications for them to manipulate.

Chapter Seven

CREATIVE DEVELOPMENT

A further area in which children develop is the realm of creativity and imagination. It's difficult to put into concrete terms exactly what imagination and creativity are: perhaps it is best to see them as a means of expressing ideas and impulses, thoughts and feelings.

People's lives are enriched through creativity, whatever form their inventiveness takes. Children's lives certainly are enhanced through their interaction with arts and crafts, music, movement, drama and so on.

Through creativity children can communicate their understanding of the world they are still trying to make sense of, particularly before they can read and write. The expression of their ideas through imaginative play, arts and crafts, using different media, can tell you a great deal about what's going on inside their heads though, of course, their creative endeavours will depend upon their level of skills.

LEARNING THROUGH CREATIVITY

When they are engaged in creative activities children are learning many things as well as how to express themselves. To begin with, they are learning to concentrate. They are learning to work on one project and do it to the very best of their ability, sticking at it until completion. They are also learning to think and are developing their thinking skills, because they're looking for different ways to get to the end they wish to achieve. They are learning to visualise something and then work out a way of achieving it.

Of course, in working at the skills they need to use, whatever their chosen project is, they are also developing their concepts of colour, shape, space, number, pattern etc so that working on any creative project in itself reinforces other learning.

THE KEY TO CREATIVITY

The real key to creativity is to get started and to have fun, to get the children to understand that there is no 'right' way and no 'wrong' way, that creativity is a completely free area for them to explore.

Rainy afternoons, when they can't play outside and they're bored with the things they have inside, are excellent times for being creative together.

THE VALUE OF CREATING

The process of doing creative things holds the real value of the activity, rather than the standard of the finished product. Particularly when you are doing creative things together, the sharing that takes place during that process is invaluable to both of you. You both learn about capabilities and thought processes by talking about what you're doing, and the children are extending their skills while they're taking part in the process.

Remember, creative activity needs to be fun – there's nothing more stifling to the creative urge than being told you are making a mess of something. The mess, or the result, is not the important thing, the means by which you go about getting to that result is the paramount purpose of the activity.

WHAT YOU NEED FOR CREATIVE ACTIVITIES

You need surprisingly few materials to embark upon creative activities and many of those can be found around the house. Many of the things you'd normally throw away as rubbish can provide an absolute treasure trove of magical bits and pieces for creative activities.

Start a small collection of things that will be useful, such as cardboard boxes, sponges, paper towel, toilet paper tubes, scraps of fabric, cardboard from packing materials, bubble wrap, magazines and brochures, paper bags, paper plates, treat-size sweet boxes, old socks and gloves, lids from cans, empty cotton reels, leftover thread and wool, yoghurt containers, cotton wool balls, old toothbrushes, scraps of wrapping paper and ribbon, coloured and transparent papers, glitter, coloured foils . . . the list is almost endless.

You can guarantee that this treasure trove will provide hours of absorbing fun activity if you just supplement it with some glue, some child scissors, a couple of felt-tip pens, Sellotape, paint-brushes etc.

You can use the 'junk' that you've saved for modelling, for collage, for montage, for just simply cutting and sticking, for painting and printing, for making puppets, for making books, even for making music.

Try to get hold of old computer paper, or wallpaper, or any large sheets of paper that you can use to cut up for painting and printing on, sticking bits and pieces to or making books out of. Children, as a general rule, are not a bit bothered about the kind of paper that's used in their creative efforts, so it doesn't have to be brand new and pristine – they're only interested in what they actually do to transform it.

HAVE SOME RULES
It might be as well to establish a few home-based rules from the outset. For example, that:

- wherever you work, you put down a cloth or an old sheet before you begin;
- everybody wears something to protect their clothes;
- you have a ten and a five-minute warning before clearing-up time;
- everything has to be cleared away, the paint-brushes washed etc before the session can be said to be over.

PRINTING
You can print with so many different objects – and the children will never cease to be interested.

Use leaves, old toothbrushes, vegetables with shapes cut into their surface, bits of sponge, left-over lids, straws etc. All you need is some thick paint poured into a saucer – if you're mixing powder paint, put a little washing-up liquid into it to make it slightly firmer.

The objects that the children are using to print with are known as the 'stamps'. They should dip the stamp into the paint to coat the surface with paint, press it firmly down on to their paper and lift it to see the print.

Sometimes it takes a little while to get the hang of lifting the stamp without it sliding across the paper

– all good for fine motor control – but with a little practice they will get it.

Get them to see how many prints they can do with just one application of the paint – what happens as they do more and more prints? How many prints can they do before the image is no longer practical – in other words, how many stamps can they make before losing the clarity of the print?

MAKING PUPPETS

There are so many different ways you can make puppets. You'd think children would get fed up with them – but they never do!

Paper plate puppets are easy. You can draw, paint, colour, and stick on bits of different materials to make a face or a head from your plate. Wool stuck on with glue makes good hair. You can even stick pieces of material to be a hat or a scarf. Then all you need to do is Sellotape a piece of card or a tube (such as a kitchen roll tube) to the back for use as a handle.

Paper bag puppets are just as simple. Paint, colour or stick the faces on to the front of the bags in exactly the same way. The bags go over your hand, and the child's hand and are secured at the wrist with some tape or a rubber band. Then your puppets can talk to each other!

You can also make puppets very easily from old socks. Make sure they're quite small socks for little hands. The sock goes on the hand and you stick on to it sticky paper eyes and any other features of the face you might want. There is your puppet!

Little treat-size sweet packets or the packets that films come in make wonderful finger puppets. Cover the box with paper first, then draw, paint or stick your face on. You can also stick arms and legs on if you wish; cut them out of cardboard and stick them on with glue.

Remember that the whole object of puppets is that they talk – they give lots of opportunity for language development – so be prepared to allow plenty of time for your puppets to talk to each other.

COLLAGES

Children will be doing a lot more than creating a work of art when they are making collages: they will be exploring textures, shapes and colours as they work out what bits and pieces they want to use in their picture.

You need to have a large sheet of paper (wallpaper or whatever) for the sheet that the collage is assembled on. Get together a collection of things that the children want to stick on. They might want to do a 'picture' that shows some kind of scene, or they might be interested in doing a collage of, for example, things that you have collected on a walk together.

Give them lots of time to sort out the bits and pieces and make their choices, because this is the crucial part of the process. Then they can decide where they want to stick the bits and the last part is sticking them on.

MONTAGES

A montage uses the same kind of idea as a collage, but it is two-dimensional, so the children should be cutting bits and pieces out of magazines, brochures or comics, and sticking them on to make some kind of satisfying picture or design. Maybe they want to do a 'red' design – so they would cut out lots of different bits of red from pictures and stick them on. Maybe they want to do a 'car' design – in which case they would cut out lots of different cars and stick them on, and so on.

MAKE BOOKS

All you need for making books is a few sheets of paper or card and some thread. Put several pieces of paper together with a piece of card for the front and back covers, punch holes through at one side and tie them together with the thread. There you have your book.

It works better if the children do the pages first, stick on their pictures or draw and colour their pictures, and you do the writing for them, if there's to be any writing.

Make a variety of books so that you have different formats – those that fasten at the top, those that fasten at the side, big ones, small ones, even very tiny ones (children love those!). You can make zigzag books by folding a piece of paper or card into a concertina shape. You have to fold this before the children do anything on the pages, of course.

Give all your books titles and put the name of the author (the child) on the front. Read the books together, and get the child to read them to the rest of the family.

JUNK-MODELLING

There's something really magical about making models out of junk! You can turn cardboard boxes into any-thing – medieval castles, garages with car parks on the roof, parks and gardens, boats, rockets to the moon, cookers, playhouses etc. Be sensitive about the results – no matter how much a chopped-up cornflakes box still looks like a cornflakes box to you, in the children's minds it is exactly what they have made it.

All you need is a bit of patience, a sharp knife or scissors and an imaginative child to tell you what to do. Obviously you need to do all the cutting yourself, but wherever the children can take over, encourage them to do so. Let them do as much of the planning and choice-making as possible – remember, it's their model, not yours (you can always make your own!), and leave them to get on with it as much as possible.

This might be difficult, because you may be enjoying yourself so much that you might want to take over, but bear in mind it is the *process* they are going through that's important, *not* the finished product.

PRESSING FLOWERS

It will take a couple of weeks to see the results of this activity, but it will be well worth it.

Pick some nice flowers from the garden (make sure they are not wet). Flat ones are best, like daisies, pansies or busy Lizzies. Try to avoid bulky flowers like roses and fuchsias.

Find something heavy, like a book, and put two layers of kitchen roll on it. Get the children to arrange the flowers on the kitchen roll. It's best if none of the flowers touch each other otherwise they will stick together as they dry. Put two more layers of kitchen roll on top. Then put lots of heavy books on top of that.

Leave the flowers for two weeks. When you go back to them they will have dried nicely. Get some good white paper and let the children arrange the flowers, gently, in a design that they like, gluing the paper before they put the petals down.

MAKING FRAMES

You can use all kinds of things to make frames for photographs or favourite pictures. Seashells work well, if you pick quite small ones. Glue the shells all round the edge of a piece of cardboard and paint them with clear nail varnish when you've finished. Try using beads, buttons, melon seeds and pasta shapes – colour them with spray paint where necessary.

MAKING MUSIC

You can make lots of musical instruments by using washing-up liquid bottles, or things like Smarties tubes, Pringles tubes etc.

Use fillings like rice, pebbles or noodles in the tubes to get different sounds when you shake them. To be really safe, stick the lids back on with superglue.

You can use various sized pots, upside-down, as drums. They will make different sounds, particularly if you bang them with different materials, for instance, metal spoons, plastic spoons etc. Sticks or pot lids banged together make different sounds again.

Children love making music and it's an important part of the creative experience. Take opportunities to sing with them, and to try to make different sounds with any real musical instruments you have and any made-up ones you can put together. Play at echoing sounds – one of you makes a rhythmic pattern of clapping or of sounds with one of your instruments and the other tries to copy the pattern.

Encourage the children to listen to different kinds of music and to talk with you about what the music makes them feel like, what it reminds them of, how they think they would like to move to it. Music creates moods and you can help your children to identify those moods just by discussing the music or by dancing to it.

IMAGINATIVE PLAY

Although very young children think in the *concrete* and *literal* way, as we have seen in Chapter Five, eventually there comes a time when you realise that they are beginning to step into imaginative or *pretend* play. They have realised that although the world is as it is, they can, in a way, step beyond it and begin to create it in another dimension for themselves.

At first they will pretend by themselves with just one toy or object but then, gradually, they will begin to include you in the play. They will begin to pretend, for instance, to be you doing the things that you do in the home, or to be their brothers or sisters being put to bed in the cot instead of the bed, or someone they have seen on the television taking part in a dramatic situation.

This progress into imaginative play is a very important part of their overall development and it means that, for the first time, they are able to think in an abstract, rather than a concrete, way.

HOW SHOULD YOU RESPOND?

You must be very careful in your responses. Hopefully it will come very naturally to you to join in with the pretence and to carry on the play. For instance, if they offer you a tub in which they have 'made you a cup of tea', take the tub and pretend to drink the tea. The first time this happens fills the children with excitement because they feel almost as if they have stumbled upon a wonderful secret and, in a way, they have!

Join in the pretence as much as you can, but remember that the children have initiated the situation and the worst thing you can do is take over and dominate it. Your sensitive involvement can lead the children to play imaginatively for longer, whereas if you try to have too much input you will devalue the game in the children's eyes.

THE PART THAT TOYS PLAY

One of the great dangers of all the toys and equipment that are available for today's children is that some of them can be so sophisticated and authentic that they require absolutely no use of the children's imagination.

A brightly-coloured plastic pedal car, for example, is always a pedal car, but a cardboard box can not only be any form of transport that the child's mind can transform it into, but also provides an opportunity for problem-solving and creating so that the box itself will look more like, and perform in some way as, the vehicle the child perceives it to be. On the other hand, something like a brightly-coloured plastic tea-set can encourage children into all kinds of role-playing games.

Really, the thing to do is to keep your own imagination open to all kinds of possibility and, where the children lead, try to follow.

DRESSING UP

Children of all ages love dressing up. The great thing about it is that they only need one item to become somebody else entirely! Keep a collection of things – hats, bags, shoes, net curtains, old dresses, jumpers, any kind of thing – and get them out periodically. You'll find that if you just leave the box or bag lying about, the children will soon delve into it and take on different roles. Again, be ready to join in and respond, to be part of the pretence.

When possible, allow the children to perform for you and other family and friends. They love 'acting the part' – either making up games or doing 'little plays' – and giving them an audience is a really good way to help them build self-confidence. Take photographs of them dressed up and role-playing. They are a good starting point to talking about feelings – what other people feel like, what it's like to pretend to be somebody else, what it feels like to be dressed as someone else.

HOW IMPORTANT IS IMAGINATIVE PLAY?

Imaginative play is crucial to children's development. Encourage this creativity – for instance, the cardboard box that may be one minute a rocket, the next minute a boat on the river, the next a mountain to be climbed. This kind of play helps them build a new perspective on the world and to understand more about what their role in the world is about. Show them that you value their imaginative play by getting involved and talking to them about it, but guard against trying to take it over. Encourage them to use the resources that you have, in ways that are unique to them.

PRACTICAL ACTIVITIES

• Do collage portraits of the whole family and display them in a gallery.

- Make a whole series of puppets and bring them together for special occasions, to act out little plays.
- Make a family book, using photographs.
- Make a 'feelie' collage – get lots of different fabrics with different textures and mingle them with bits of sandpaper, tinfoil, feathers etc.
- To make a clear collage, get some laminating paper from a hardware shop and cut out a sheet. Pull off half of the backing, arrange lots of different objects on it, and then pull off the rest of the backing and stretch it over the top to protect the collage surface.
- Make books about colours, numbers, names, people in the family, friends, favourite food, favourite toys etc.
- Make 'families' out of eggshells, using felt pens to draw faces. Glue on scraps of wool or thread for hair.
- Use pressed flowers and leaves to make a birthday card for someone.
- Use finger paints to create an entire family of crocodiles or alien monsters.
- Make jigsaws. Choose a picture you like. Spread glue over a piece of card which you've cut to the same size. Put the picture on the card, taking care to get rid of any wrinkles. Place it between two sheets of paper and put heavy objects on top to stop it curling up as the glue dries. When it's dry, cut the picture into an appropriate number of pieces.
- Make concertina people. Fold some paper into zigzags. Draw an outline of a person on the front, making sure the arms come right to the side of the paper. Cut around the person, but don't cut where the arms end. Open it up. Draw in all the people's features. Do this with teddy bears etc, instead of people.

Chapter Eight

OFF TO NURSERY

It can be quite frightening, sending your children off to nursery or playgroup for the first time. It's frightening for them and it's frightening for you. But the path is so much smoother for both of you once you are prepared.

WHAT CHILDREN WORRY ABOUT

The things that frighten children about going off into the big, wide world for the first time are:

• leaving you – will you still be there at the end of the day? Will you remember to come and fetch them? Will everything carry on as normal after going to 'school'?;
• making friends – how will they make friends? Will the other children like them? Will the adults/teachers like them? Will *they* like the others? What if they're too shy to speak to anyone?;
• doing things – will the tasks and activities be too hard for them? Will they fail miserably? Will everyone else be much better and much cleverer than them?;
• independence – how will they manage if they need the toilet quickly? What if they have an accident? What if they don't get a drink? What if they lose their coat or forget which is their peg?

121

What Parents Worry About

The things that frighten parents about children going off into the big, wide world for the first time are:

- leaving them – will they cry/scream/have a tantrum? Will they sob through the whole of the session? Will they ever trust you again?;
- making friends – how will they get on? Suppose all the other children know each other and are friends already? What if *your* child is the one that gets left out of everything? Will they be rejected by the adults for some little personal habit or trait you've overlooked?;
- doing things – will the tasks and activities be so far beyond them that they give up at the first hurdle? Will they understand the instructions? Will they be willing to *try*? Will all the other children be much better and much cleverer than them?;
- independence – will they manage to get to the loo in time? What will happen if they have an accident? What will happen if they need a drink? Maybe they'll lose their coat or bag or forget which is their peg . . .

. . . and so on. You can see that the worries of the children and the parents are basically the same, just seen from a different perspective. What is more, *most* children's worries and *most* parents' worries are the same, and the pre-school groups are well equipped to deal with them!

Settling In

Even though they sob when Mum or Dad passes them

over, the majority of children really do stop the moment he or she's out of sight and they're happily playing away with toys or activities they've never seen before.

If the transition is difficult and they don't settle down, you might be invited to hang on for a while the next time, and help them to settle down yourself. The drawback of this can be that it encourages the child to be clingy and unhappy but if the group leader thinks it's necessary and you have the time, don't be worried about it. Try to be as reassuring as you can and take the first chance of getting away. Once children know their mums or dads are definitely coming back to collect them, they usually relax.

MAKING LIFE EASIER

You can do a lot of things to make life at the nursery or playgroup easier for them. To begin with, children need to feel that they are as much in control as they possibly can be. For this reason they need to feel confident in being able to cope on their own with using the toilet, with taking drinks or eating, with washing their hands, removing their outer clothing and putting it back on again, removing their shoes for physical development or creative movement sessions, and things like that.

Sometimes it's hard to 'let go' and encourage them to practise doing all these things for themselves at home, not least because it's very time-consuming and there's usually a mad panic to get out on time every morning. But the only way they will feel confident in their independence is in practising it.

HOW YOU CAN HELP THEM BECOME MORE INDEPENDENT

• Praise them for their efforts to manage with their clothing, help with the really fiddly bits, and give them lots of opportunity to keep trying for themselves.

• Try to make things easier for them – why make life more difficult than it needs to be? Shoes with velcro fastenings are much easier for them to manipulate than those with straps and buckles or laces. Zips on jackets are quite difficult to manoeuvre when you're only just developing fine motor control – pulling the zip up is OK, but getting it fixed into its homing at the bottom is the difficult part. Joggers or leggings with elastic waists are quicker to pull down if you need the loo in a hurry than jeans or dungarees with braces and belts. All of these things, once you think about them, will help to increase their independence and their confidence in their own ability.

• Make sure that they know what the routines are: that they join the group for registration, that they follow instructions, that they needn't be afraid to tell someone when they need the toilet or whatever, that they have a drink and a biscuit and perhaps another settling down altogether session before home time. You'd be surprised how secure these little routines make children feel, and how much happier they are when they can predict what's going to happen next.

RELUCTANCE TO GO TO NURSERY

Most children start nursery or playgroup quite happily

because they look forward to playing with lots of other children, and because, if you've already been on a visit, it looks very exciting with lots of toys and activities they've never tried before.

However, some children are not always quite so keen.

THE SHY CHILD

Shy children can't ever be 'talked out' of their shyness, so there's no point in trying. What you have really got to do is try to make them feel more confident.

The first step towards this is by not laughing at the shyness. Talk about it openly so that they know you understand. Tell them, 'It's OK to be shy sometimes, I understand what it feels like, it happens to me.'

Don't insist that they talk to other children: if you say, 'Maybe you could just say "hello",' and leave it at that, they might achieve that – what to you seems a very simple – goal. Praise them for what is, for them, a very real achievement.

Talk to the group leader about the problem. Shy children cannot bear to be 'in the spotlight' with everybody staring at them. Activities where they are called out in front of the group to sing to everyone or talk about 'news' are enough to put them off for life. Try to ask the group leader if they can handle such situations with sensitivity. Often these tasks can be avoided until your child feels more confident.

Confidence comes when you feel good about yourself and happy in the situation you are in. Think of ways you can build up their self-esteem. In such circumstances it is more important than usual to talk about the group routines, the other children and the adults who are there, so that they know what's going to happen and who's going to be there.

THE FRIGHTENED CHILD

All children are afraid at some point. It doesn't matter how irrational the fears are, logic won't prevent them.

Sometimes it is something in their own imagination which frightens them – for instance, they might see the nursery rabbit in its hutch as a ferocious wild animal that's going to attack them. Sometimes they are afraid of other children – not for any particular reason, but maybe they've seen a child lose its temper or get out of control, and it worries them.

Sometimes they're afraid of the fact that they are not as strong or powerful as the other children or adults who surround them. They feel that others have more *authority* than they do and wonder what will happen if they do something wrong.

Children can be frightened of tangible things – paint on their hands or their clothes, a bee or fly in the room, a wobbly toilet seat – all kinds of things that you might tell them are 'silly'. Try to remember that however un-founded the fears are to you, they are very real to them.

Children are seeing the world from their own perspective and are still trying to make sense of it in their own way. So all they have to bring to that interpretation is what they have already learned and what they have already experienced.

To help conquer your child's fears you need to understand them, to show that you respect your child and give constant reassurance. Tell him/her over and over again that he/she'll be able to cope, that everything will be all right in the end. Don't try to avoid meeting the fears because your child needs to face up to them to see that he or she can overcome then. Help him/her to relax and breathe more easily so that they are not so tense, and give lots and lots of praise for every small step they make towards conquering their fears.

KEEP THE GROUP INFORMED

Children may face many traumas in their early years – illness, hospitalisation, the death of a beloved pet, the person who's been caring for them full-time returning to work, family break-up etc. If you know there is something happening at home which is upsetting, take the first opportunity to tell the group leader or one of the helpers, so that they can keep an eye on the children and if necessary help them to talk their way through their problems. The majority of nursery and playgroup leaders are only too happy to give children going through hard times a supportive back-up in 'real' ways, by keeping them closer if necessary, getting them to be their 'helpers', holding their hands or giving them extra hugs if it looks as if they're going to get upset, and so on.

HOW TO PREPARE YOURSELF

The more you know about how nursery and other pre-school groups work, the better equipped you are to know what's going to happen to your children when they're out of your sight and control.

All pre-school groups, including nursery schools,

nursery classes, day nurseries, playgroups etc, see themselves as partners with parents and carers in children's pre-school education. The idea behind the pre-school groups is not that they take the children over or take them away from their parents or carers to 'educate' them, it's that the children's education is a continuous process which incorporates the whole of their experience – at home, at the group, at other places.

The aim of pre-school groups is, therefore, to involve you in as many ways as they can. They don't want to alienate you from your children, but to add on to what your child has learned from you at home. They need your help to provide the children with lots of pre-school experience that will build up concepts, skills and good attitudes. After all, you have more influence on the children at home than they will ever have at the group. Thus, if you can reinforce what they are teaching, the children will learn more effectively.

For this reason, most groups are at pains to form a partnership with you, right from the beginning.

WHY YOU SHOULD HELP TO FORM THAT PARTNERSHIP

One of the big obstacles to learning is a feeling of emotional insecurity. Children can feel insecure for all kinds of different reasons – they may feel physically unwell, they may feel alienated and alone, rejected, afraid, unsure of what's happening or what they are meant to do.

One of the things that makes them feel apprehensive is if their parents or carers don't 'get on' with their teacher or disagree with what the school or group is doing. It gives them a feeling of divided loyalty. When they are at the group they need to feel a bond with the leader and helpers, so that they feel physically and emotionally safe. But if their parent or carer frequently voices misgivings or antagonistic opinions about their group, children do not know quite how to respond. Should they do what the group leader wants, or what the parent wants?

On the other hand, if you show that you value good, strong links with home, and you support everything that happens in the group and all those looking after it, the children will feel completely at ease and will learn more effectively.

WORKING WITH THE GROUP

A good group will go out of its way to try to involve parents and carers, and to make them feel as if the group is a solid part of the neighbourhood community. Ways in which they might try to do this are:

- getting to know parents and children before they come into the group. They will try to do this in different ways – perhaps by setting up visits to see the group working before the children enter; perhaps by visiting your home to discuss the children's progress and their needs; perhaps by having occasional meetings to which parents are invited, where they discuss what they are going to teach; perhaps by starting a parents' group;
- encouraging parents to play an active part in the children's education. They will do this by providing you with as much information as possible, and showing you how certain subjects or aspects of the

curriculum are tackled, by asking you to help the children to continue with tasks and activities at home and by showing you how you can do so;

• giving parents a clear overall explanation of what they are doing, why they are doing it, and what their aims are. Most groups will provide a written 'Welcome' booklet or brochure, giving the group's philosophy, aims and objectives. They will make sure that there are opportunities for informal discussion with you on a regular basis and help you to see the connection between what they are doing and what the children achieve. They will try to be sensitive to the needs of the children and the parents, and will be anxious to smooth anxieties or solve problems before they get too much of a hold;

• regularly communicating. As well as the methods mentioned in previous points, a good group will send letters home with the children that are brief, well written and informative. They will have a parents' notice-board and make sure that all notices displayed are up-to-date, look neat and fresh, and give all the necessary information;

• socialising. There will be times when the parent group is encouraged to organise social events, perhaps in order to fundraise, or merely as a get-together. There are also times, such as on Celebration Days, when parents and carers will all be invited into the group to share in the events.

If you find it difficult to become involved in any of these ways because of other commitments, be perfectly honest with the group. Apologise that although you would love to be involved and do more, it's just an impossibility for you at the moment. Ask them to please let you know if there are any ways in which you can help. All groups are open to offers of help – even if it is only saving and washing empty yoghurt pots for activities, it shows you have their interests at heart.

WORKING TOGETHER

Your involvement is helpful to your children, in as many ways as you can possibly make it. To begin with, if you can connect yourself to the group in some small ways you will learn more about what's going on, simply by observation and casual conversation. You will develop a growing appreciation of how young children learn and you will be in a prime position to observe how the children are making progress. Certainly there are more opportunities for you to be in touch with what is happening at the group than there will ever be after your child has started formal schooling and, in a way, you may feel a closer link with the nursery or playgroup than you will ever feel with the much more formal school sector.

Try to build on the group's welcoming approach. It's important to try and make it to the first gathering, but if you can't make an introduction or meeting at the time that you're first offered, no one will get upset if you explain and ask for another appointment.

Don't ever be afraid to ask questions – it shows your interest and lets the group know that you're anxious to have a bit of background knowledge, and this is all good for the children. If you can get off to a good, friendly start it will hold you in good stead for the next twelve months or two years.

131

WHAT PRE-SCHOOL GROUPS TEACH

The education of pre-school children in nurseries and playgroups is not left to chance. Every group that works with children of pre-school age in the private, voluntary and maintained sectors now has to work in accordance with a document published by SCAA (School Curriculum and Assessment Authority) called *Nursery Education – Desirable Outcomes for Children's Learning*.

The Desirable Outcomes are goals for learning which the children should reach by the time they enter compulsory education, before or during the term after their fifth birthday. All children are expected to make maximum progress towards the Outcomes so that they'll be well equipped to work towards Key Stage One of the National Curriculum by the time they begin school.

THE DESIRABLE OUTCOMES

The nursery or playgroup curriculum is organised into six sections. These are:

• Personal and Social Development – making friends, sharing, having confidence, being independent, knowing right from wrong;
• Language and Literacy – speaking and listening, reading and writing;
• Mathematics – numbers, shape and space, measuring;
• Knowledge and Understanding of the World – science, history, geography, information technology;
• Physical Development – motor skills and control;

• Creative Development – imagination, art and craft work, dance, music.

Each of these key sections has very clear written aims and objectives, which are detailed in the document. These aims are all at the children's level so, for example, an objective in Knowledge and Understanding of the World, for history, might be 'to talk about past and present events in their own lives'. In plain English, this might mean that a small group of children would have a session where they talk about who's had a birthday this week, who had one last week, who has one to come. While they were having this talk session, they would also, simultaneously, be fulfilling an objective of Language and Literacy, which would be 'to listen attentively and talk about their experiences'. They would, at the same time, be fulfilling an objective in Personal and Social Development to 'establish effective relationships with other children and adults'.

Every nursery or group's planning for each school term and year has to be written down in accordance with these goals and be shown to be working towards them. You can be sure that any activities your children are engaged in during their pre-school group experience are designed to lead towards the goals of the Desirable Outcomes in one or more of the six sections.

PARENTS AS PARTNERS
One of the features of the Desirable Outcomes document is a section called 'Parents as Partners'. It outlines the ideal groups should be aiming for and recognises the importance of the parents' role in pre-school education.

BASELINE ASSESSMENT

When they begin at a pre-school group, all children are to be assessed on what is known as a Baseline Assessment standardised test. At the time of going to print the proposals for Baseline Assessment have not been quite finalised, but assessments will be made more or less in relation to the Desirable Outcomes, using its sections as 'testing' areas. In other words, each child will be assessed for their grasp of concepts, skills and attitudes within those areas.

This is not as shocking as it sounds! 'Baseline' basically means 'starting point', and the assessment is really to find out where the children are when they enter the group and, therefore, how much progress they make while they are with the group. Although the information will help groups and schools to monitor children's development, it is also very helpful in deciding whether the groups themselves are doing a good job – and they are to be inspected regularly to make sure that the work they are doing is strictly in line with the Desirable Outcomes.

Most groups will probably try to assess their children once a term. Their findings will help them to identify where children have needs, what those needs are, and how they can supply them.

For example, children who are being assessed in Language and Literacy may be observed to see if they can: (Speaking and Listening), sit quietly and listen to a story, follow a simple instruction, volunteer responses to discussion and initiate conversation with peers and adults; (Reading), hold a book appropriately, turn

pages appropriately and tell a story from memory;
(Writing), understand that print has meaning, use
symbols and identifiable letters in communication and
write their own name with appropriate letters.

If they can't do any of these things their assessment
sheet will be marked to show it, and the teachers will
know that these are areas they will have to work on
with those children before the next term's assessment.
If they can do these things or more, then, again, their
learning behaviour will be observed, the assessment
sheets marked as appropriate, and plans will be made
to move the children on to further goals.

How You Can Help

Usually the children will not have any idea they are
being assessed because the evaluations will be made
by informal discussion and observation, the teacher
marking the assessment sheets afterwards. So rather
than being *tested* they are being offered opportunities to
show what they have already learned.

You can help by working with them at home in the
ways already explained in this book, so that they do
their activities naturally and with confidence during
the time they are at the group. The more they have
done with you at home, the more likely it is that they
will quite naturally fulfil the requirements of Baseline
Assessment without any bother.

The one thing you need not do is feel worried about
Baseline Assessment. It is not so much a test of the
children or of you as an evaluation to give the teachers
an idea of how to plan progression into the activities
and tasks that they want the children to do. If you

begin to feel anxious about Baseline Assessment you will quite naturally feed that anxiety to the children who will become worried about 'failing'. Baseline Assessment is not really about 'failing' or 'succeeding', it is about recognising what is already in place, and what is needed.

WHAT TO DO IF YOU THINK YOUR CHILD HAS SPECIAL NEEDS

'Special needs' is the overall term which is used for children who have some kind of delay or impairment that prevents them from learning or developing as quickly as other children of their age.

These needs may take the form of: hearing difficulties or impairment; visual difficulties or impairment; physical difficulties, delay or impairment; speech and language difficulties; learning difficulties – poor memory/recall/perceptual skills; medical conditions; emotional/behavioural difficulties or giftedness.

You have to remember that all children are individuals and that each will develop at their own rate. However, sometimes it becomes apparent that a child is not making any progress at all in particular areas. What you have to look at is whether the child in question has *significantly* more difficulty in learning than most children of the same age.

This difficulty may arise in any, or more than one, of the areas given above. Your first port of call, if you are worried yourself, is always your local Health Visitor or your GP, who will first assess the child themselves and then bring in, or refer the child to, further experts in the different areas of need, to get a considered opinion and secure the appropriate help for the child. If the group leader has noticed problems before you have, she/he may ask you to see your GP. Remember, she/he will be giving this advice with your child's interests at heart.

Try to be true to your own instincts. Parents, particularly mothers, often have intuitive feelings when there is something not quite right – if this is how you feel, don't allow yourself to be 'fobbed off' or reassured and sent away, because every moment that an assessment or diagnosis is not made, is a moment lost that could be very valuable to the child.

Different health and education authorities have different provision available for children with special needs. If you find yourself in the position where you need outside help, please try to get hold of as much support and guidance as you can, from every source that you can. You will often find there is help and assistance available to you that is not actually offered unless you ask for it (money!), and you have every right to fight for your child and for your needs.

SEN CODE OF PRACTICE

SEN stands for Special Educational Needs. All groups and schools have to work to a document produced by the Department for Education, called the 'Code of Practice on the Identification and Assessment of Special Educational Needs'.

The Code of Practice requires them to access outside help from physiotherapists, speech therapists, medical experts, educational psychologists, social services etc, and you're entitled to this expert help for any child that has those special needs.

HOW ASSESSMENT WORKS

Children are to be assessed in a place where they and the family can feel comfortable, and you have to be informed, at every stage of the proceedings, what is happening and what the intentions are for follow-up. Your own feelings should be taken into account and you should not be afraid to ask any questions. Please do not feel that you are betraying your own lack of awareness by asking questions – what you are trying to do is *find out more*!

STATEMENTING

If it turns out that the child being assessed has a profound problem or disability, a 'statement' has to be written. It is very rare for statements to be written for children under the age of two but their progress will be carefully monitored and, hopefully, lots of outside, even home-based help will be made available to you.

Basically, a statement is what it says it is: a statement of the child's special educational needs. It sets out exactly what provision the child needs, and what provisions the LEA, health services, social services and other agencies *are obliged to make* in order for that child to learn.

The statements of children under the age of five are expected to be informally reviewed at least once every six months to make sure that the provision made is still appropriate to the child's needs and you should be kept informed and involved at every stage.

Appendix

Useful Addresses

Advisory Centre for Education (ACE)
1b Aberdeen Studios, 22/24 Highbury Grove,
London N5 2EA

Association For All Speech Impaired Children (AFA-SIC)
347 Central Markets, Smithfield, London EC1A 9NH

British Association for Early Childhood Education
111 City View House, 463 Bethnal Green Road,
London E2 9QY

Disability Information Centre
Middlesborough General Hospital,
Ayresome, Green Lane, Middlesborough,
Cleveland TS5 5AZ

Exploring Parenthood,
Latimer Education Centre,
194 Freston Road, London W10 6TT

Gingerbread (For One Parent Families)
49 Wellington Street,
London WC2E 7BN

National Association for Special Educational Needs
NASEN House, 4/5 Amber House,
Business Village, Amber Close,
Amington, Tamworth, Staffs.

National Campaign for Nursery Education
23 Albert Street, London NW1 7LU

National Centre for Play
Moray House, Institute of Education,
Crammond Campus, Crammond Road,
Edinburgh EH4 6JD

Network for the Handicapped
16 Princeton Street, London WC1R 4BB

National Playbus Association
AMF House, Whitby Road, Bristol BS4 3QF

Tumble Tots (gymnastics for babies and toddlers), for
information on your nearest centre call 0121 585 7003.

For more information on the Desirable Outcomes for
Children's Learning, call 0345 543 345 and ask for the
parents' booklet.